Exam Grade Booster: IGCSE Chemistry Edexcel

Liam Porritt, Jason Lee & James Alvey

Checked and Approved by:

Richard Brookes
Senior Deputy Head, City of London School
M.Chem & D.Phil, Chemistry
University of Oxford
Examiner for two international exam boards

James Fisher
Teacher of Chemistry, Tonbridge School
BSc (Hons), Chemistry
University of Nottingham
Examiner for three international exam boards

Kevin O'Riordan
Director of Studies, Holmewood House School
BSc (Hons), Chemistry, HDipEd
University College Cork
IGCSE Chemistry tutor

Christopher Lawrence
Head of Chemistry, Tonbridge School
MA (Hons) & PhD, Natural Sciences
University of Cambridge
A-level Chemistry examiner

Greg Fisher
Chemistry Teacher, Tonbridge School
BSc (Hons), Chemistry & MA (Dist.), Science Education
University of London
Expert examiner for international exam board

Published by Exam Grade Booster
(Publisher prefix 978-0-9930429)
www.examgradebooster.co.uk
First Edition published 2016

ISBN-13:   *978-0-9930429-4-2*

Disclaimer
The author and named checkers and approvers of this publication give no guarantee of improved examination performance nor will they be held responsible for any mistakes which may appear in this publication. They are not responsible if this publication, in any way, has a detrimental effect on its reader(s) or any other persons. This publication offers suggestions which have produced results for the author, but does not in any way state that these methods are the only ways of succeeding in IGCSE examinations.

CONTENTS

ABOUT THE AUTHORS

LIAM PORRITT

I have been extremely fortunate to attend one of the best schools in the country and in this book I aim to share the outstanding, exam-focused teaching that has led to my success. I believe my experience and knowledge of revising for and then taking IGCSE examinations make this guide uniquely suited to preparing any student for success in their own Chemistry exams.

It has taken me over three years to produce this guide, and even then I had to recruit the help of two similarly driven students to ensure the guide was as good as it could possibly be. My first guide, *Exam Grade Booster: GCSE French*, received extremely positive reviews, The Independent Schools' Modern Languages Association calling the book 'a very worthwhile purchase: wholeheartedly recommended'. I have no doubts that this guide will prove equally useful for anyone studying IGCSE Chemistry. My goal is to share with everyone the techniques and tricks I have learnt while studying Chemistry, particularly those which others can emulate in both the revision process and the exam room itself.

JASON LEE

Having been lucky enough to be taught by some fantastic teachers, and having experienced what a dramatic effect they had on raising my grades, I strongly believe that academic success is *not* only reserved for the naturally able. I have witnessed the power of the drive to succeed – something you must have if this book is to help you – in conjunction with the high-quality, exam-specific learning materials that we aim to provide in this book. By coauthoring this guide with Liam and

James, I hope to produce a resource that not only contains all of the information you need to learn, presented in a student-friendly style, but also to do so in the most concise manner possible so that you can maximise your revision efficiency. Having begun to write this guide shortly after our IGCSEs, we believe we are better equipped to identify and address common areas of misunderstanding and carelessness. This has allowed us to produce the ultimate revision guide – one that we wish we'd had when we were in your shoes!

JAMES ALVEY

For me, writing this guide was not just about producing an amazing tool to help you climb up the grade ladder, it was also about trying to write a chemistry guide that students actually find interesting! A great deal of success is based on interest; you are significantly more likely to be willing to give time for an activity if you enjoy it. So, as well as providing the tools and information you need to succeed in your IGCSE chemistry exams (Liam & Jason made sure that there is plenty of this!), a great focus was put on asking the right questions and sparking an interest in the reader. Essentially, getting the  student to ask "why?" in the first place is, in my opinion, a great start. I hope this guide goes at least some distance towards achieving this goal, providing more engaging content that makes it easier to push towards higher grades.

ABOUT THE CHECKERS & APPROVERS

The checkers and approvers of this book are all qualified teaching professionals. Between them, they have over 70 years of teaching experience, all of them having taught or tutored Edexcel IGCSE Chemistry. They all share the authors' goal of providing students in any schooling environment access to the same superb, exam-driven advice.

HOW TO USE THIS BOOK

So that you can boost your grade, this book will enable you to...

UNDERSTAND KEY IDEAS	Understand the basic principles behind each section, as this will help you to remember pieces of information more easily. It will enable you to manipulate what you know to suit the question being asked and will also give you a chance of working the answer out if you can't remember a fact or if you haven't seen a similar question before.
LEARN THE FACTS	Ensure you know all of the information that you will need to use in your answers by learning and testing yourself on our questions. These questions include all of the facts required and by actively revising them in our guide, you will be well prepared to answer any exam-style question that comes your way!
USE THE 'BUZZ-WORDS'	Maximise the number of marks you score on harder questions by using your chemistry knowledge appropriately, and answering the question efficiently by using the correct 'Buzz-Words' (words which are on the examiners' mark scheme). If you do that, the examiner will have no choice but to give you the marks. These are contained within all of the answers given.
MANIPULATE YOUR KNOWLEDGE	Know how to manipulate your knowledge by answering exam-style questions. Seeing and then doing questions similar to the ones you will be presented with in your exam will enable you to get used to using your knowledge so that it appropriately answers a specific question. This will help you find out exactly what sort of answers the examiners will be looking for. Similar questions come up year after year – all you have to do is slightly manipulate your knowledge to make sure that you answer the question being asked! **We've also thrown in some 'weird' (and hopefully more entertaining) questions to really test your understanding with the key concepts presented throughout the book.**

This book is designed to boost your chemistry GCSE or IGCSE grade, and is suitable for both double and triple science candidates.

The areas that are only necessary for those doing triple science are indicated and made obvious by being enclosed in this **grey box with a vertical dotted line**. In the 'Learn' and 'Manipulate' sections, triple science questions will be marked by a '*'.

Concepts that we believe are particularly important to know are highlighted using a **light blue box**.

Later in the book, **purple boxes** are used for calculations.

GOLDEN RULES
THESE ARE VERY IMPORTANT CONCEPTS OR POINTERS TO BE AWARE OF.

The contents of the syllabus will be divided into five sections covering each of the overarching sections of the syllabus. Each chapter is divided into three different components that, together, will ensure you are as well-prepared as possible. They are clearly marked out throughout the course of the guide and are as follows:

✓ **UNDERSTAND** – this will provide you with a clear and relatable explanation of the theory behind each of the areas of chemistry in your exam. This understanding will be crucial on the day in allowing you to use the information you have learnt to answer the specific question in front of you rather than just writing down information related to the section being examined. It will also facilitate your learning of the key facts by putting that information into a context that you comprehend. It is crucial you read and understand each chapter, and if you have any problems in understanding anything, read it again, and if you are still uncertain, don't be afraid to go and ask your teacher.

✓ **LEARN** – these are quick-fire tests found at the end of each chapter to help you actively learn essential facts and figures. The questions are given with the answers below, bullet pointed so that you know exactly where each mark would be awarded.

There is then a list of exactly the same questions at the back of the guide (starting on **pg. 183**) that you should use to test yourself, ensuring you follow these steps for the best results possible:

1. Once you have gone through a chapter's 'Understand' section, (such as the one on 1.1 – 'States Of Matter'), highlighting and annotating key information, you should attempt to memorise the answers to the learn questions for that chapter.

OUR TIP

Test yourself on the questions in a totally random order, writing down each question number as you answer each question. This is crucial, as it will ensure you are learning the information rather than the sequence in which it appears.

2. Turn to the 'Learn' questions presented without the answers at the back of the book (starting on **pg. 183**) and, using a piece of paper, attempt to answer all of the questions for that chapter.

3. Mark your answers and be tough on yourself! Even if you were very close or got most of it right, mark it wrong. Then, try to memorise anything that was incorrect. If you got them all right, congratulations! You can skip to step 6.

4. Redo all of the questions you didn't get 100% correct from that chapter, again doing them in a different order from last time. Mark them and carry on retesting yourself on any you keep getting wrong until you get them all correct. Then, test yourself on the whole chapter again; hopefully you'll get them all right this time. If not, retest yourself on the ones you got wrong until you can answer all of the questions correctly, in a random order, in one go.

5. Move onto the next chapter's 'Understand' section and follow steps 1-4 for that chapter. Continue until you have completed all of the 'Learn' questions for an entire section (such as 1.1, 1.2, 1.3, 1.4, 1.5 & 1.6).

6. Within a week of completing all of the chapters, you should attempt to answer all of the 'Learn' question for an entire section. Follow the above procedure, testing yourself on the whole section, retesting yourself on any you get wrong and then testing yourself again on the whole section until you can answer all of the questions correctly.

7. Once you have learnt the answers to all of the questions from every section, it is a good idea to test yourself on questions from random chapters every so often to make sure you don't forget any of the key information! If you find you particularly struggle with a couple of chapters the first time around, focus on retesting yourself on these before revisiting other chapters.

OUR TIP

Test yourself on questions from a random subsection in a random order. Do all of the questions from a subsection (e.g. 1.2 – Atomic Structure), before moving onto the questions from another subsection (e.g. 1.5 – Covalent Substances) in a random order, and so on.

This may seem like a whole lot of steps, but it's really not that complex once you've had a go at it a couple of times. What is more, it is definitely worth the effort as this method guarantees you know all of the key facts and figures needed for your exam!

✓ **MANIPULATE** – these questions will test both your ability to manipulate the facts you have learnt and your understanding of these facts, presenting you with exam-style questions that draw on material from an entire section. They will also prepare you for questions that may come up in your exam.

This manipulation of your knowledge will also be greatly improved by doing past papers, so once you have completed all of the sections in this guide, we strongly recommend you complete at least 3 past papers under exam conditions to familiarise yourself with the style and length of the papers you will be taking.

Some Last Words...

The very last section of this book (Section 6) focuses on how you can best use the knowledge you will acquire in the rest of this guide to ensure you obtain the best mark possible on the day of your exam. The 'Common Mistakes' section is particularly important and highlights all the mistakes that we found ourselves and our peers making when practicing for the exam. If you know what to look out for you shouldn't make the same mistakes!

Section 1:

Basics, Atomic Structure & Bonding

1.1: STATES OF MATTER

Here, we will be learning to:

☑ Describe and explain the arrangement and movement of particles in solid, liquid and gaseous state, and the interconversions between these three states.

☑ Investigate dilution and diffusion using experiments.

✓ UNDERSTAND

Matter is arranged in three distinct ways that characterise how it behaves and its properties. The difference between the three for a given material is associated with the **kinetic energy** (movement energy) in the **particles:**

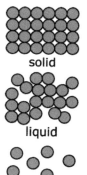

- **Solids:** have a **regular arrangement** consisting of particles which vibrate about **fixed positions** within a **lattice** formation. This is the **lowest** energy state. The particles are not free to move over one another, and as such the material has a fixed shape.

  solid

- **Liquids:** have an **irregular arrangement** consisting of particles which are free to move over one another but do not have enough energy to entirely escape the attractions holding them together. Hence, liquids are incompressible (like solids).

  liquid

- **Gases:** have an **irregular arrangement** consisting of particles of the **highest energy** of the three states. The particles have sufficient energy to mean that they are completely separated from one another. They move in straight lines, changing direction when they collide with other particles or with the walls of the container.

  gas

INTERCONVERSIONS BETWEEN SOLID, LIQUID AND GAS

Most substances can be converted between the three states - for example, water.

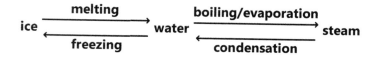

ice $\xrightarrow{\text{melting}}$ water $\xrightarrow{\text{boiling/evaporation}}$ steam

with reverse arrows labelled **freezing** (ice ← water) and **condensation** (water ← steam)

The solid form of water is **ice**. If we supply the water molecules with **heat energy**, they gain **kinetic energy** such that they vibrate more about their fixed positions. Once they have enough energy to break some of the **intermolecular attractions**, they can shift from their positions and flow over one another, resulting in a **liquid water** state. This familiar process is known as **melting**.

OUR TIP

Intermolecular forces refer to attractive forces between molecules.

On the continued supply of heat energy, the particles reach a stage where they completely overcome the intermolecular attractions of the other molecules, becoming free to move throughout the container. This results in **steam**, being formed from the **boiling/evaporation** of the liquid water.

Evaporation does not require the water to reach its boiling point (100°C). If the water particles gain enough energy from the surrounding environment, they can still escape the 'body' of liquid. Thus, evaporation of water can occur at **any temperature** (boiling only occurs when water reaches 100°C or over). Evaporation occurs only at the **exposed surface** of the liquid to the air (boiling occurs throughout the liquid, leading to bubbles forming in the liquid), and is a **much slower process**.

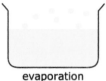

evaporation

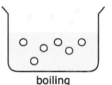

boiling

The reverse occurs in the other direction: **cooling**. Gas particles lose kinetic energy and slow down, eventually reaching a stage where the intermolecular attractions overcome the energy of the moving particles and they are once again bound in the liquid state. This process is **condensation**. The final stage involves a further decrease in energy of the particles to a point where the attractions are strong enough to hold them in their fixed positions, **freezing**.

Sometimes a solid transitions straight to a gas (this is rare), called **sublimation**. An example would be **dry ice** in theatres, which involves solid carbon dioxide transitioning to carbon dioxide gas. The opposite of this is **deposition**.

If we plot the temperature of the water against time, we get **heating** and **cooling curves** that look like these:

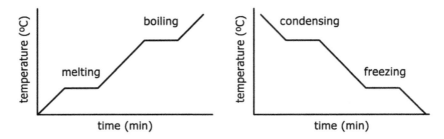

You may have noticed that the temperature remains constant while the water is changing state. Why does this happen? Well, as the water molecules change state with increasing temperature, **intermolecular forces** between the water molecules are being broken. To break these forces, energy needs to be put in. We say such a process is **endothermic**. As a result, for a period of time during the change of state, the energy we supply is not actually increasing the kinetic energy of the water molecules. Instead, the energy is being used to break the bonds. Therefore, because there is no increase in the kinetic energy of the molecules, there is no change in temperature. As for cooling, intermolecular forces form as the water changes state. Energy is released into the surrounding environment as these intermolecular forces form between water molecules. This process makes it **exothermic**.

DIFFUSION

Diffusion occurs when particles move from a region of high concentration to one of low concentration. We can demonstrate this: fill a gas jar with brown bromine gas, and invert a second, empty gas jar to seal the opening of the first. Over time, the bromine molecules will eventually diffuse from the bottom gas jar to the rest of the apparatus.

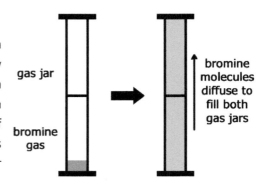

The process is slow because liquid and gas particles move about in what is termed **Brownian motion** - the constant random movement of particles caused by collisions with other particles, which are also in continuous and random motion.

DILUTION

Dilution is the reduction of concentration in a solution. We can demonstrate this by dissolving around 158g of purple potassium manganate(VII) in 1000cm^3 of water to give a deep purple solution. If we take 100cm^3 of the solution and add another 900cm^3, we will now have on average, 15.8g of potassium manganate(VII) dissolved in 1000cm^3 of water. We can see that this second solution has a much lighter purple than the original solution. This is due to a reduction in the concentration of the potassium manganate(VII) solution. Even if we kept diluting the solution, we would still be able to see (to some extent) a hint of purple, showing the presence of potassium manganate(VII) ions. Eventually, the solution will be so diluted that we won't be able to perceive colour. Nevertheless, even though there does not appear to be a colour we know there is still a massive number of particles of manganate ions per cm^3. This gives us an idea of how small particles really are.

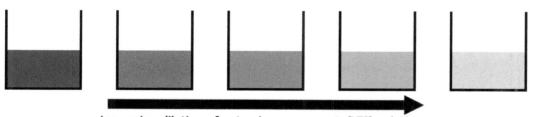

increasing dilution of potassium manganate(VII) solution

✓ LEARN

1. Describe the arrangement and movement, and draw the structure of particles in:

a) A solid [1]

> ✓ **Particles are closely packed in a regular arrangement and vibrate about fixed positions.**

b) A liquid [1]

> ✓ **Particles are still touching but are less regularly packed than in solids and can slip and slide over one another.**

c) A gas [1]

> ✓ **Particles are much further apart, are arranged randomly and move in straight lines.**

2. What is Brownian motion? [1]

> ✓ **The constant random movement of tiny particles (e.g. smoke particles) caused by collision with (invisible) air or water molecules, which are themselves in continuous and random motion.**

3. How can you show that a sample of water is pure? [1]

> ✓ **The substance will boil at 100°C and freeze at 0°C if the substance is pure water.**

4. What is the name of the process by which substances move from an area of high concentration to an area of low concentration? [1]

> ✓ **Diffusion**.

5. The following experiment is set up. Answer the following questions:

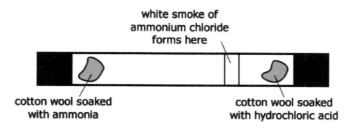

white smoke of
ammonium chloride
forms here

cotton wool soaked
with ammonia

cotton wool soaked
with hydrochloric acid

a) Why would particles of hydrochloric acid and ammonia move towards each other? [1]

    ✓ **Both substances are diffusing away from their respective cotton wools (where concentration is high) and towards the opposite end (where concentration is low).**

b) The white smoke is formed when both substances react. Which substance (ammonia or hydrochloric acid) moves faster and why? [2]

    ✓ **The ammonia particles move faster than hydrochloric acid particles as the ammonia particles are lighter, but have the same energy.**

    ✓ **This conclusion is drawn because the white smoke that forms is closer to the hydrochloric acid end than the ammonia end. This means the ammonia particles have travelled a greater distance in the same time.**

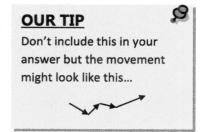

OUR TIP

Don't include this in your answer but the movement might look like this...

1.2: ATOMIC STRUCTURE

Here, we will be learning to:

☑ Define the terms atom, molecule, element, compound, mixture, atomic number, mass number, isotope and relative atomic mass.

☑ Describe the structure of an atom.

☑ State the relative charge and relative mass of a proton, an electron and a neutron.

☑ Use the periodic table to deduce the atomic number, mass number, neutron number and electron configuration of given element.

☑ Explain why elements of the same group display similar chemical properties, and why Group 0 elements are inert.

✓ UNDERSTAND
· ·

Some definitions:

- **Atom:** the smallest individual unit of an element that shows all the properties of that element.
- **Molecule:** a particle containing two or more atoms chemically bonded together, and is the smallest particle in an element or compound that shows all the properties of that element/compound.
- **Element:** a substance which cannot be broken down into anything simpler by chemical means, and contains atoms of only one type.
- **Compound:** a combination of two or more *different* elements chemically bonded together in a fixed ratio.
- **Mixture:** a collection of two or more substances (elements or compounds) which can be physically separated.

The atom consists of...

- **Electron shells** - energy 'levels' which contain electrons orbiting around the nucleus. The most important shell is the outer shell (the **valence shell**), since it is involved with electron transfer during chemical reactions, essentially determining the outcome of each particular chemical reaction.

- **Nucleus** - which is made up of **protons** and **neutrons**, but (despite the diagram, which is not drawn to scale) is tiny compared to the size of the whole atom (the atom is 1×10^{-10} m across; the nucleus is 50000x smaller).

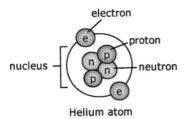

Helium atom

	Relative Charge	Relative Mass
protons	+1	1
neutron	0	1
electron	-1	~1/2000

THE PERIODIC TABLE

The Periodic Table shows all the known elements in **ascending order of atomic number**. Each square on the Periodic Table looks like this:

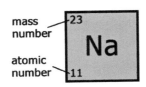

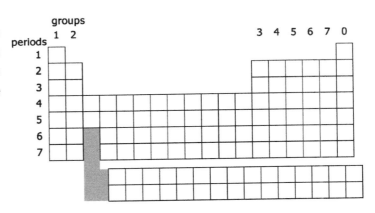

- **Atomic number:** number of protons. For an element, the **number of protons = number of electrons** (**I repeat:** FOR AN ELEMENT ONLY).
- **Mass number:** number of protons + neutrons.

We can use this information to infer other things about the element:

---

number of neutrons = mass number - atomic number

In this example, sodium (Na) has 11 protons and 23 - 11 = 12 neutrons.

ELECTRON CONFIGURATIONS

As far as IGCSE Chemistry is concerned, you only need to derive the **electron configurations** (i.e. number of shells, and electrons in each, for a given element) for the first 20 elements of the Periodic Table. We can use information from the Periodic Table to do this:

OUR TIP

The innermost shell can only hold up to 2 electrons; the 2nd can hold up to 8, and the 3rd can hold up to 18 (although you'll only be required to fill up to 8 electrons in the 3rd shell).

- The **group number** shows the number of electrons in the outer shell.
- The **period number** shows the number of electron shells.

For example, the electron configuration of Na would be: 2, 8, 1.

Reactions are all about stability. As far as this guide is concerned, this is expressed by the statement that all atoms *want* to have a **full outer shell of electrons**. Atoms react with other atoms in order to achieve this, by a process of electron transport, forming **bonds**. A **bond** is essentially an attraction between something that is positively charged and something negatively charged (an **electrostatic attraction**) which then proceeds to bind the two atoms. The two different types of charge are created due to the movement of electrons, placing an abundance of negative charge in one area and leaving a deficiency of negative charge in another area, resulting in a positive charge.

GOLDEN RULE
ATOMS 'WANT' A FULL OUTER SHELL OF ELECTRONS TO GAIN STABILITY.

Group 0 elements are known as the **noble gases** - they are **inert** (unreactive) because they already have full outer shells and so do not need to gain/lose electrons in order to become stable.

ISOTOPES AND THE RELATIVE ATOMIC MASS

Isotopes are atoms of the same element with the **same number of protons** but a **different number of neutrons**.

OUR TIP

The number of valence electrons determines the chemical properties of an element.

They are of the same element because they share the same number of protons (i.e. they have the same atomic number). They also **do not differ in chemical properties** because they contain the same number of electrons in the outer shell.

Because isotopes differ in mass numbers (due to differences in the number of neutrons), the relative abundance of each naturally occurring isotope is taken into account to calculate the **relative atomic mass** of a given element.

The **relative atomic mass (A_r)** is the weighted average mass of an atom of an element, taking into account its naturally occurring isotopes, relative to 1/12th the mass of an atom of carbon-12. The last part of the definition basically means that all mass numbers are compared to that of 1/12th the mass of an atom of carbon-12. For example, helium atoms have an A_r of 4, which means on average, they weigh the same as 4/12ths the mass of an atom of carbon-12.

So, where we previously said that, when you look at the periodic table, the number above an element's atomic symbol is its mass number, this was not quite correct - it is just often said to simplify things. In fact, the number above an element's atomic symbol is its relative atomic mass. Don't worry too much about exactly how to calculate the relative atomic mass for now, as we'll get onto that on Section 5. It's just important that you understand the difference between the mass number of an isotope and the relative atomic mass of an element.

✓ LEARN

1. Explain what is, and give an example of:

   a) An element [2]

   > ✓ **A substance which cannot be broken down into anything simpler by chemical means.**
   > ✓ **E.g. Fe - or anything on the Periodic Table.**

   b) A compound [2]

   > ✓ **Two or more elements chemically combined.**
   > ✓ **E.g. H_2O**

   c) A mixture [2]

   > ✓ **Two or more substances which are not chemically combined and can be physically separated.**
   > ✓ **E.g. sand and water**

   d) An atom [2]

   > ✓ **Smallest part of an element that shows all the properties of that element.**
   > ✓ **E.g. Fe - or anything on the Periodic Table (REJECT: any diatomic element unless written as a single atom e.g. reject 'O_2', accept 'O').**

2. Fill in the gap. *The number of _____ must remain the same for the element to remain the same.* [1]

   > ✓ **The number of <u>protons</u> must remain the same for the element to remain the same.**

3. The diagram below was taken from a Periodic Table and shows information on silver:

a) State the number of protons in an atom of silver. [1]

  ✓ **47**

b) State the number of neutrons in an atom of silver. [1]

  ✓ **108 - 47 = 61 neutrons**

4. Fill in the table using the Periodic Table **(pg. 205)**: [7]

Element	Mass Number	Protons	Neutrons	Electrons
	106	46	60	
Silicon	28			14
	65	30		

Element	Mass Number	Protons	Neutrons	Electrons
Palladium	106	46	60	**46**
Silicon	28	**14**	**14**	14
Zinc	65	30	**35**	**30**

5. What is shown by an element's...

a) Group number (if the element was in Groups 1-7)? [1]

  ✓ **The number of electrons in its outer shell**

b) Period? [1]

    ✓ **The number of electron shells (levels) around the nucleus occupied by electrons**

6. Use the Periodic Table **(pg. 205)** to work out which element has 2 electrons in its outer shell and a total of 5 electron shells. [1]

    ✓ **Strontium**

7. Use the Periodic Table **(pg. 205)** to deduce which element has a combined total of 72 electrons and protons. [2]

    ✓ $\frac{72}{2}$ **= 36 = number of protons = number of electrons**
    ✓ **Krypton (award both marks if only correct element given).**

8. Where in the atom are protons and neutrons found? [1]

    ✓ **Nucleus**

9. State the relative masses and charges of an electron, a neutron and a proton. [6]

    ✓ **Electron - Relative Mass: 1/2000**   **Relative Charge: -1**
    ✓ **Neutron - Relative Mass: 1**   **Relative Charge: 0**
    ✓ **Proton - Relative Mass: 1**   **Relative Charge:+1**

10. What do helium, neon and argon have in common about their outer electron shells? What effect does this have on their chemical reactivity? [2]

    ✓ **They all have full outer shells.**
    ✓ **They are inert (they do not react).**

1.3: SEPARATION METHODS

Here, we will be learning to:

☑ Understand the purposes of filtration, crystallisation, chromatography, simple distillation and fractional distillation.

✓ UNDERSTAND

FILTRATION

Filtration is used for separating an insoluble solid from a liquid, or a soluble solid from an insoluble one. For example, sand can be separated from water by pouring the mixture down a funnel with filter paper. The sand will collect at the filter paper as the particle sizes are too big to fit through the gaps in the filter paper. (i.e. it is the **residue**). The resulting mixture of filtered substances is called the **filtrate**.

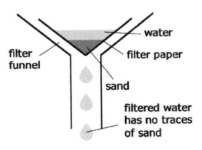

CRYSTALLISATION

Crystallisation is mainly used for purification. Impure salt crystals can be dissolved in a warmed solvent such as water. Any insoluble impurities can be removed by filtration. The filtrate is then cooled, allowing pure hydrated crystals to form. These crystals are then filtered from the solvent and dried using two pieces of filter paper.

> **OUR TIP**
>
> **'Soluble'** means it can be dissolved. The solid that dissolves is a solute. The liquid it dissolves in is the **solvent**. The whole system (solute dissolved in solvent) is referred to as a **solution**.

CHROMATOGRAPHY

Chromatography can be used to separate liquids, based on their differences in solubility in a given solvent. It can be shown in a simple **chromatogram** setup. One basic example would be separating out different pigments that make up an ink colour.

One could prepare a beaker filled with a small amount of water, draw a dot of ink on a piece of filter paper, and place that in the beaker, such that the level of the water starts below the dot. The water would soak through the filter paper and reach the ink. Different dyes have different solubility levels in water. As the water moves up the filter paper, it separates these different dyes. How far the dye moves up the paper depends on:

- How strongly it sticks to the paper.
- How soluble it is with the solvent.

The dye that is most soluble in the solvent and sticks least to the filter paper moves up the paper quickest. We can make some measurements to calculate the R_f **value**:

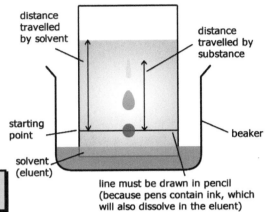

distance travelled by solvent

distance travelled by substance

starting point

solvent (eluent)

beaker

line must be drawn in pencil (because pens contain ink, which will also dissolve in the eluent)

$$R_f = \frac{\textbf{distance travelled by substance}}{\textbf{distance travelled by solvent}}$$

One can find out the composition of the mixture by comparing the R_f value calculated to **reference values** of known substances using the same chromatogram. Furthermore, spots at the same height are probably the same chemical substance.

SEPARATING IMMISCIBLE LIQUIDS

Immiscible liquids do not dissolve in each other, meaning when you mix them together, they separate into different layers (e.g. try mixing water with oil). To separate immiscible liquids, we place them into a **separating funnel**. After some time, the two liquids will separate into different layers – the liquid with the higher density will form the lower layer. By opening the tap, we can allow the bottom liquid to run out of the funnel into a beaker.

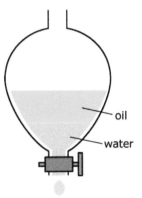

oil

water

Once most of the water has been collected, we tap off some liquid into a spare beaker until oil is running out of the funnel. We then collect the oil in a third beaker.

SIMPLE DISTILLATION

Simple distillation is ideal for separating miscible substances (mixes well) with large differences in their boiling points.

An example would be separating water from a salt solution. The salt solution can be heated to around 100°C so the water will boil and leave the solution as water vapour. The water vapour will then condense back to liquid water within the condenser (which has cold water running outside it).

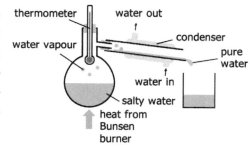

FRACTIONAL DISTILLATION

Fractional distillation is a more complex form of distillation, and is used to separate liquids with more similar boiling points. These liquid mixtures are typically more miscible, thus, requires a more complex method of separation. It differs from simple distillation in that a **fractionating column** is included which aids separation.

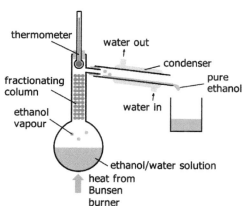

An example would be separating ethanol from water. Ethanol has a lower boiling point than water (~78°C) and so the heating is monitored to ensure that the temperature does not reach 100°C (the boiling point of water). Ethanol evaporates and travels up the fractionating column, before condensing when it enters the condenser. Water also evaporates but is more likely to condense in the fractionating column.

✓ LEARN

....

1. Name a suitable method for obtaining:

   a) Water from a table salt solution. [1]

      ✓ **Simple distillation**

   b) Water from a mixture with any insoluble solid. [1]

      ✓ **Filtration**

   c) An amino acid mixture, in which each amino acid has a different level of solubility. [1]

      ✓ **Chromatography**

   d) Obtaining petrol from a mixture of petrol and kerosene. [1]

      ✓ **Fractional distillation**

2. Kenny finds some impure copper(II) sulfate crystals which he wishes to purify. Describe the steps he should take to do so. [5]

   ✓ **Use hot water to dissolve the crystals and stir with a glass rod.**
   ✓ **Filter to remove insoluble impurities.**
   ✓ **Heat to allow some of the water to evaporate off then cool to allow crystallisation.**
   ✓ **Pure hydrated copper(II) sulfate crystals will precipitate.**
   ✓ **Filter out these crystals and dry them between two pieces of filter paper.**

1.4: IONIC COMPOUNDS

Here, we will be learning to:

☑ Deduce the charge of an ion formed from an element belonging to any of Group 1, 2, 3, 5, 6, and 7.

☑ Define an ionic bond.

☑ Describe the formation of an ionic bond, and illustrate the process using dot and cross diagrams (for Groups 1, 2, 3, 5, 6 and 7 elements only).

☑ Define oxidation and reduction in terms of electrons.

☑ Describe and explain the properties of ionic lattices.

☑ Explain the relationship between ionic charge and melting/boiling point.

☑ Draw the structure of a sodium chloride crystal.

✓ UNDERSTAND

As mentioned in Section 1.2, atoms lose or gain electrons to attain stability (i.e. gain a full outer shell), and this can mean reacting with other atoms.

- For **Groups 1-3** elements, this usually involves atoms losing enough electrons to 'empty' the outermost shell. The full electron shell before the outermost shell would then become the new 'outer' shell. In reactions, we say they become **oxidised** (they lose electrons).
- For **Groups 5-7** elements, this usually involves atoms **gaining** enough electrons to fill their outer shell. We say they have become **reduced** (they gain electrons).

For example, sodium (Na) has 1 electron on its outer shell. To attain a full outer shell, it must lose this electron, becoming oxidised. We write the ion as **Na$^+$** (because it now has 1 more proton than electron, so it has a net charge of +1).

> **OUR TIP**
> Remember **OILRIG** - Oxidation Is Loss of electrons, Reduction Is Gain of electrons

- Groups 1-3 elements form **cations** (positive ions) with charges of +1, +2 and +3 respectively.

- Groups 5-7 elements form **anions** (negative ions) with charges of -3, -2 and -1 respectively.

Compound ions contain more than one element (you do not need to know why) - they have fixed charges that you will need to learn.

Ammonium NH$_4^+$
Hydroxide OH$^-$
Nitrate NO$_3^-$
Sulfate SO$_4^{2-}$
Carbonate CO$_3^{2-}$
Phosphate PO$_4^{3-}$

FORMING AN IONIC BOND

When a metal and a non-metal react, a series of processes take place:

1. The metal loses electrons to gain a full outer shell. It becomes a positive ion (i.e. a cation).
2. The non-metal gains electrons from the metal to gain a full outer shell. It becomes a negative ion (i.e. an anion).
3. The two oppositely charged ions attract (via **electrostatic attraction**) and bond. This chemical bond is called an **ionic bond**.

This can be illustrated using a **dot and cross diagram**. For example, let's look at the reaction between magnesium (Mg) and oxygen (O):

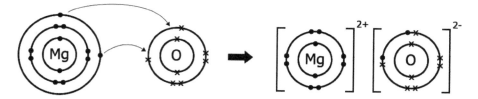

We know from the Periodic Table that Mg is a Group 2 metal - it has 2 electrons in its outer shell that it needs to lose; and that O is a Group 6 non-metal - it has 6 electrons on its outer shell, so it needs to gain 2 more. Once the Mg loses its 2 electrons to the O, both form oppositely charged ions (Mg^{2+} and O^{2-}) which then attract one another, thus forming the ionic bond.

GOLDEN RULES
YOU MUST INCLUDE THE CHARGES (OUTSIDE THE SQUARE BRACKETS) ON THE RESPECTIVE IONS WHEN DRAWING THEM OUT.

What about instances where both elements need to gain/lose a different number of electrons than one another to gain a full outer shell? For example, in a reaction between beryllium (Be) and fluorine (F), Be needs to lose 2 electrons but F only needs to lose 1. In this case, the electrons from Be can fill the shells of two F atoms:

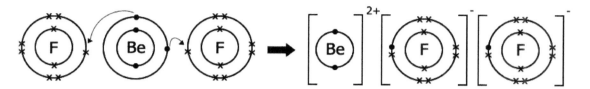

Because you needed one Be^{2+} ion to balance two F^- ions, the chemical formula of the resulting beryllium fluoride product would be **BeF_2**.

PROPERTIES OF IONIC LATTICES

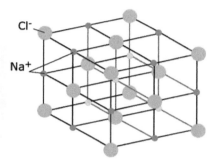

An **ionic lattice** is a giant 3D lattice structure held together by the electrostatic attractions between oppositely charged ions. Sodium chloride (NaCl) for example looks like this (right) - each ion is ionically bonded to six others, and it takes on a cubic shape:

This structure gives ionic compounds the following properties:

- **High melting and boiling points** because lots of energy is required to overcome the strong electrostatic attractions between the oppositely charged ions.
- **Soluble in water** - because each ion is charged, it can be 'pulled apart' by water molecules.
- **Can conduct electricity when molten or in solution** because the ions become mobile. A current is after all, a flow of charge, and ions are charged particles.

There is a relationship between melting and boiling point depending on the size of the charge of the two ions in an ionic lattice. The higher the ionic charges, the higher the melting/boiling points due to **greater electrostatic attractions** between the positive and negative ions. These require more energy to overcome.

✓ LEARN

1. Draw a dot and cross diagram to show the ions formed after a reaction between sodium and oxygen. [2]

     ✓ **1 mark for correct ions, including charges**
     ✓ **1 mark for correct numbers of each ion (i.e. 2 Na and 1 O)**

   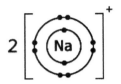

2. Draw the ionic lattice of NaCl.* [2]

     ✓ **1 mark for cubic shape.**
     ✓ **1 mark for showing Na⁺ ion surrounded by six Cl⁻ ions.**

   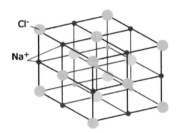

   OUR TIP

   It's hard to draw, but you basically want to show that each Na^+ ion is bonded to six Cl^- ions, demonstrating some form of a 3D cubic structure.

3. Which of MgO or NaCl has the higher melting point and why?* [2]

     ✓ **MgO because of the stronger electrostatic attractions between the higher charged Mg^{2+} and O^{2-} compared to the Na^+ and Cl^- ions.**
     ✓ **Thus, more energy is needed to overcome the electrostatic attractions within MgO than NaCl.**

4. Write down the chemical formula of the product formed from a combination of NH_4^+ and Cl^-; Na^+ and SO_4^{2-}; Al^{3+} and O^{2-}; and Cu^{2+} and NO_3^-. [4]

     ✓ **NH_4Cl**
     ✓ **Na_2SO_4**
     ✓ **Al_2O_3**
     ✓ **$Cu(NO_3)_2$**

   OUR TIP

   Use brackets around ions involving more than one type of atom.

1.5: COVALENT SUBSTANCES

Here, we will be learning to:

☑ Understand covalent bonding as a result of electrostatic attractions between a shared pair of electrons and the protons in the nuclei of the atoms involved in covalent bond.

☑ Recall the positions of metals and non-metals in the Periodic Table.

☑ Illustrate covalent bonding using dot and cross diagrams for hydrogen, chlorine, oxygen, nitrogen, hydrogen chloride, water, carbon dioxide, methane, ammonia, ethene and ethane.

☑ Describe the properties of substances with simple molecular structures and giant covalent structures.

☑ Draw the structures of diamond and graphite.

☑ Explain how the structure of diamond makes it suitable for cutting, and the structure of graphite for lubricating.

☑ Explain why graphite can conduct electricity.

✓ UNDERSTAND

If the reaction is between **two non-metals**, the atoms still want to gain full outer shells, but one of the two atoms cannot **lose** electrons since it would be further away from having a full outer shell, not closer. Therefore, together the two atoms **share** a pair electrons and form what is called a **covalent bond.**

A covalent bond forms because of the electrostatic attraction between a **shared pair** of electrons (negatively charged) and the protons (positively charged) in the nuclei of the bonding atoms.

hydrogen

The Periodic Table on the following page shows the position of the non-metals. **Do not worry about metalloids** - they show some characteristics of both metals and non-metals. For IGCSE's sake, the orange line divides metals from non-metals.

groups

periods	1	2											3	4	5	6	7	0
1	H																	He
2	Li	Be											B	C	N	O	F	Ne
3	Na	Mg											Al	Si	P	S	Cl	Ar
4	K	Ca	Sc	Ti	V	Cr	Mn	Fe	Co	Ni	Cu	Zn	Ga	Ge	As	Se	Br	Kr
5	Rb	Sr	Y	Zr	Nb	Mo	Tc	Ru	Rh	Pd	Ag	Cd	In	Sn	Sb	Te	I	Xe
6	Cs	Ba		Hf	Ta	W	Re	Os	Ir	Pt	Au	Hg	Tl	Pb	Bi	Po	At	Rn
7	Fr	Ra		Hf	Db	Sg	Bh	Hs	Mt	Ds	Rg	Cn	Uut	Fl	Uup	Lv	Uus	Uuo

- metal
- metalloid
- non-metal
— line separating metals from non-metals

La	Ce	Pr	Nd	Pm	Sm	Eu	Gd	Tb	Dy	Ho	Er	Tm	Yb	Lu
Ac	Th	Pa	U	Np	Pu	Am	Cm	Bk	Cf	Es	Fm	Md	No	Lr

DOT AND CROSS DIAGRAMS OF EVERYTHING

You can represent covalent bonds using dot and cross diagrams. Below is a list of diagrams you need to learn (though if you understand everything taught so far, you should be able to work them out!):

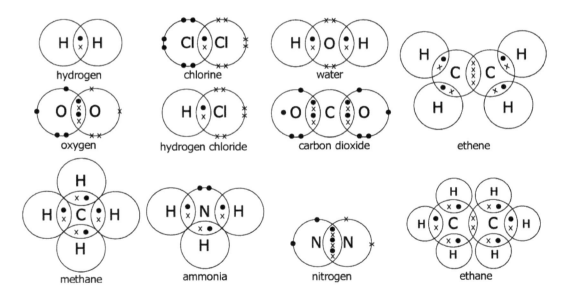

hydrogen   chlorine   water   ethene

oxygen   hydrogen chloride   carbon dioxide

methane   ammonia   nitrogen   ethane

H_2, Cl_2 and N_2 are examples of **diatomic elements** (which also include O_2, F_2, Br_2 and I_2). They exist as two atoms of the same element covalently bonded together.

PROPERTIES OF SIMPLE MOLECULAR STRUCTURES

Compounds with covalent bonds typically form **simple covalent structures**, with properties including:

- **Low melting and boiling points** due to the **weak intermolecular forces** that require little energy to be overcome. However, the covalent bonds between the atoms in a molecule are **strong**.
- They are **poor conductors of electricity** because there are **no charged particles** to carry the current.
- They tend to be **insoluble in water** but **soluble in organic solvents**.

GIANT COVALENT STRUCTURES

Giant covalent structures are giant structures whereby the covalent bonds extend through the compound. Diamond and graphite are examples, both of which are allotropes of carbon (**allotropes** are different forms/arrangements of the same element in the same physical state).

Diamond consists of carbon atoms, each forming four covalent bonds with adjacent carbon atoms, to form a **giant 3D tetrahedral lattice**. Its properties:

each C bonded to four others...

- The naturally **hardest** material in the world due to its strong, tetrahedral arrangement, making it ideal for use in **cutting**.
- A very **high sublimation point** due to the need for vast amounts of energy to break many strong covalent bonds.
- **Does not conduct electricity** because it has no mobile charged particles.

Graphite consists of carbon atoms each only forming covalent bonds to three carbon atoms. This results in **flat hexagonal layers**. It also leaves each carbon atom with a **'non-bonded' electron**. This electron is **delocalised** (i.e. able to move), allowing graphite to conduct electricity.

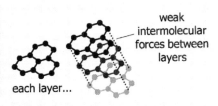

weak intermolecular forces between layers

each layer...

Its properties:

- Like diamond, it has a **high sublimation point** for the same reasons.
- It **conducts electricity** due to each carbon having a mobile electron.
- It has a **layered structure**, with weak intermolecular forces between each layer. This means the layers can slide off each other. This property makes graphite an ideal **lubricant**.

Obviously, you are not expected to be able to draw perfect diagrams of both diamond and graphite. If asked to do so in the exam, make sure you mentioned the key features of the structures (i.e. the correct number of bonds, the shape...etc.). You can get away with drawing something similar to the diagrams shown below:

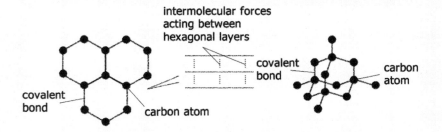

GOLDEN RULE

WHEN SIMPLE COVALENT SUBSTANCES MELT OR BOIL, IT IS THE WEAK INTERMOLECULAR FORCES BETWEEN THE MOLECULES THAT ARE BROKEN, NOT THE COVALENT BONDS. WHEN GIANT COVALENT SUBSTANCES MELT OR BOIL, IT IS THE COVALENT BONDS THAT ARE BROKEN.

✓ LEARN

1. Define a covalent bond. [1]

    ✓ **A covalent bond is the electrostatic attraction between a shared pair of electrons and the protons in the nuclei of the bonding atoms.**

2. Why is Cl_2 a gas at room temperature? Explain with respect to its structure and bonding. [2]

    ✓ **Weak intermolecular forces between the Cl_2 molecules (which take on a simple molecular structure)...**
    ✓ **Do not require much energy to overcome.**

3. Draw the dot and cross diagram for methane. [1]

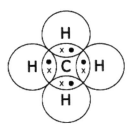

4. Why do diamond and graphite have such high melting points?* [2]

    ✓ **Both are giant covalent structures.**
    ✓ **Vast amount of energy is needed to break the many strong covalent bonds extending throughout these structures.**

5. State a use each for diamond and graphite.* [2]

    ✓ **Diamond can be used for cutting.**
    ✓ **Graphite can be used as a lubricant.**

1.6: METALLIC BONDING

Here, we will be learning to:

☑ Describe the structure of metals.

☑ Explain the properties of metals, including melting/boiling points, electrical conductivity and malleability.

✓ UNDERSTAND

Metals are giant structures consisting of a **lattice of positive ions** surrounded by a 'sea' of **delocalised electrons**. The metallic bonds form due to attractions between the positive ions and the delocalised, negative electrons.

PROPERTIES OF METALS

The structure of metals gives them some characteristic properties:

metal

- **High melting and boiling points** due to the strong electrostatic attraction between the positive ions in the lattice and the delocalised, negative electrons.
- **Good conductors of electricity** due to the delocalised electrons, which can move.

alloy

- **Good conductors of heat** because heat will cause the delocalised electrons to vibrate more, and these can transfer energy throughout the whole metal.
- **Malleable** - they can be bent and shaped because the regularity of the positive lattice means that the layers of ions can slide over one another without breaking the metallic bonds. **Alloys** (which consist of a mixture of metals) are less malleable because the positive lattice will contain metal ions of different sizes. Larger ions can prevent the sliding of smaller ions.

✓ LEARN

1. True or false? "The following elements are metals: **a)** boron; **b)** lithium; **c)** neon; **d)** rubidium; **e)** zinc; **f)** iodine." [6]

   - ✓ **True: b) d) and e) (1 mark each).**
   - ✓ **False: a) c) and f) (1 mark each).**

2. Describe the bonding in magnesium. [1]

   - ✓ **Giant lattice consisting of positive Mg^{2+} ions surrounded by delocalised electrons.**

3. Why can copper conduct electricity? [1]

   - ✓ **Its structure consists of delocalised electrons which can move throughout the whole structure.**

4. Why are metals malleable? [1]

   - ✓ **The layers of ions can slide over one another without breaking the metallic bonds.**

5. Why are alloys less malleable? [2]

   - ✓ **The positive lattice consists of different sized ions.**
   - ✓ **Larger ions prevent the sliding of smaller ions.**

✓ SECTION 1: MANIPULATE

(Total: 34 marks)

These questions will require you to utilise what you know from multiple chapters of this section. Try your best!

1. What is:

   a) An ionic bond? [1]
   b) A covalent bond? [1]
   c) A metallic bond? [1]

2. Why do metals conduct electricity and what makes them so malleable? [2]

3. Which has the higher melting/boiling points, sodium chloride or water, and why?* [3]

4. Graphite and diamond are both **giant covalent** structures.*

   a) Draw the structure of:
      i.   Graphite [1]
      ii.   Diamond [1]

   b) Fill in the blanks: *Diamond and graphite are both made up of _____ atoms but they are arranged differently in the same physical state (i.e. they are _____). [2]*
   c) Explain why diamond and graphite have very high melting and sublimation points. [3]
   d) Graphite is a good lubricant. Explain why. [1]
   e) Diamond is used for cutting. Explain why. [1]

   f) Buckminsterfullerene is another allotrope of carbon. It has the formula C_{60} and the structure of one molecule is shown to the right. Is buckminsterfullerene simple molecular or giant covalent, and why? [2]

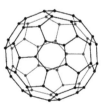

5. State the chemical formulae for:

    a) Magnesium sulfate [1]
    b) Magnesium chloride [1]
    c) Sodium bromide [1]
    d) Calcium oxide [1]
    e) Calcium carbonate [1]
    f) Potassium nitrate [1]

6. Describe what happens in terms of electrons when lithium and chlorine react. [3]

7. Describe what happens in terms of electrons when sodium and oxygen react. [3]

8. Draw a dot and cross diagram of H_2O, showing outer electrons only. [1]

9. Why does Br_2 exist as a liquid at room temperature when it takes so much energy to break the Br-Br covalent bonds? [2]

SECTION 2:

REACTIONS & WRITING EQUATIONS

2.1: WRITING EQUATIONS

Here, we will be learning to:

☑ Write word equations.

☑ Balance chemical equations.

☑ Understand state symbols in balanced chemical equations.

✓ UNDERSTAND

....

We now have some idea of how metals and non-metals react, but how do we represent these reactions? Equations illustrate the starting point and result of a reaction.

WORD EQUATIONS

Literally with these, all you need to do is get the reactants and products spelt correctly. Here is a word equation for example - it's very easy:

magnesium + water → magnesium hydroxide + hydrogen

CHEMICAL EQUATIONS I: BALANCING CHARGES

You know the equation in word form, now you need to convert it into chemical form. However, before you balance the equation, you must get the chemical formulae of the reactants and products right! The chemical formulae for elements are easy (just find them on the Periodic Table). As for compounds...

GOLDEN RULE

BALANCE CHARGES FOR COMPOUNDS.

Let's revisit the equation above. We know from the Periodic Table and from our knowledge of diatomic elements that:

$Mg + H_2O →$ magnesium hydroxide $+ H_2$

But what is the chemical formula for magnesium hydroxide? We know from previous chapters that magnesium only needs to lose 2 electrons to form a full outer shell, thus becoming a +2 ion (Mg^{2+}).

We also know the chemical formula for hydroxide ions is OH^- and that these have a charge of -1.

So we need 2 x OH^- ions to cancel out the +2 charge of an Mg^{2+} ion. Thus, the formula for magnesium hydroxide is $Mg(OH)_2$.

$$Mg + H_2O \rightarrow Mg(OH)_2 + H_2$$

CHEMICAL EQUATIONS II: BALANCING EQUATIONS

The three of us used to be taught by this one teacher who always said: *"The one and only rule of balancing equations is that they **must** balance."*

It's so unhelpful yet so true. What goes in must come out.

OUR TIP
1. Work out what the reactants and products are in word form.
2. Replace the words with their chemical formulae.
3. Balance the equation.

GOLDEN RULE
THE NUMBER OF ATOMS OF EACH ELEMENT ON EITHER SIDE OF AN EQUATION MUST BE THE SAME.

Looking back at our equation:

$$Mg + H_2O \rightarrow Mg(OH)_2 + H_2$$

On the left we have: 1 x Mg, 2 x H and 1 x O atoms.
On the right we have: 1 x Mg, 4 x H and 2 x O atoms.

We need 2 more H and 1 more O atoms on the left. This can be done by doubling H_2O:

$$Mg + 2H_2O \rightarrow Mg(OH)_2 + H_2$$

Now everything balances out! One thing to note:

GOLDEN RULE

WHEN BALANCING EQUATIONS (WHERE THE REACTANTS AND PRODUCTS ARE CORRECT), YOU CANNOT ADD OR REMOVE REACTANTS/PRODUCTS TO BALANCE THE NUMBER OF ATOMS FOR EACH ELEMENT.

In other words, you can't do something like this:

$$\times \quad Mg + H_2O + 2H + O \rightarrow Mg(OH)_2 + H_2$$

CHEMICAL EQUATIONS III: ADD STATE SYMBOLS (BUT ONLY IF ASKED)

State symbols show the physical states of the reactants and products:

$$Mg(s) + 2H_2O(l) \rightarrow Mg(OH)_2(aq) + H_2(g)$$

(s) – solid	**(l) – liquid**	**(aq) – aqueous solution**	**(g) – gas**

IONIC AND HALF EQUATIONS

Half equations are used to illustrate the changing of electrons in a reaction or in electrolysis. You only really need to understand what they mean and how to write them for use in quantitative electrolysis calculations which will be shown in Section 5 **(pg. 137)**. Here are two equations:

$$Cu^{2+}(aq) + 2e^- \rightarrow Cu(s)$$
$$Mg(s) \rightarrow Mg^{2+}(aq) + 2e^-$$

The first equation shows that the Cu^{2+} ion has gained 2 electrons (i.e. has been reduced) to form solid Cu. The second equation shows that the Mg has lost 2 electrons (i.e. has been oxidised) to form Mg^{2+} ions.

If you add the left hand sides and the right hand sides of the two equations together and cancel out the 2e⁻ vertically, you get the overall **ionic equation**:

$$Cu^{2+}(aq) + Mg(s) \rightarrow Cu(s) + Mg^{2+}(aq)$$

The main rule for ionic equations is that the **charges must balance**.

WHAT ABOUT TRANSITION METALS?

Transition metals are highlighted in the Periodic Table and can form a wide range of stable charged ions (e.g. Cu^+, Cu^{2+}...etc.). The tend to form **coloured salts**!

The charge of the transition metal ion is denoted by a **roman numeral in brackets** (e.g. copper**(I)** oxide Cu_2O and copper**(II)** oxide CuO) Assume they form +**2 ions** unless told otherwise.

However, you do need to recall that **Ag⁺** and **Zn²⁺** form **+1 ions**.

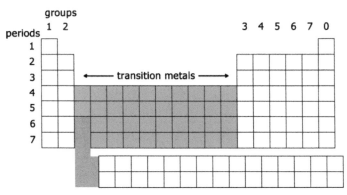

✓ LEARN

1. Write down the chemical formula for the following:

   a) Sodium carbonate [1]

   ✓ Na_2CO_3

   b) Calcium oxide [1]

   ✓ CaO

   c) Iodine [1]

   ✓ I_2

   d) Aluminium chloride [1]

   ✓ $AlCl_3$

   e) Ammonium hydroxide [1]

   ✓ NH_4OH

   f) Potassium manganate(VII) (**hint:** manganate ion is MnO_4^-) [1]

   ✓ $KMnO_4$

2. Balance the following equations:

   a) $H_2 + O_2 \rightarrow H_2O$ [1]

   ✓ $2H_2 + O_2 \rightarrow 2H_2O$

b) $H_2SO_4 + NaOH \rightarrow Na_2SO_4 + H_2O$ [1]

    ✓ **$H_2SO_4 + 2NaOH \rightarrow Na_2SO_4 + 2H_2O$**

c) $Al^{3+} + e^- \rightarrow Al$ [1]

    ✓ **$Al^{3+} + 3e^- \rightarrow Al$**

d) $Li + HCl \rightarrow LiCl + H_2$ [1]

    ✓ **$2Li + 2HCl \rightarrow 2LiCl + H_2$**

e) $C_6H_{12}O_6 + O_2 \rightarrow CO_2 + H_2O$ [1]

    ✓ **$C_6H_{12}O_6 + 6O_2 \rightarrow 6CO_2 + 6H_2O$**

3. Rewrite the following word equations as balanced chemical equations:

a) potassium + water → potassium hydroxide + hydrogen [1]

    ✓ **$2K + 2H_2O \rightarrow 2KOH + H_2$**

b) hydrochloric acid + magnesium hydroxide → magnesium chloride + water
(**hint:** hydrochloric acid is HCl) [1]

    ✓ **$2HCl + Mg(OH)_2 \rightarrow MgCl_2 + 2H_2O$**

c) calcium + water → calcium hydroxide + hydrogen [1]

    ✓ **$Ca + 2H_2O \rightarrow Ca(OH)_2 + H_2$**

d) sodium carbonate + nitric acid → sodium nitrate + water + carbon dioxide (**hint:**
nitric acid is HNO_3) [1]

    ✓ **$Na_2CO_3 + 2HNO_3 \rightarrow 2NaNO_3 + H_2O + CO_2$**

2.2: GROUPS 1 & 7

Here, we will be learning to:

☑ Describe and explain the trend in the reactivities of Group 1 metals.

☑ Describe the reactions of lithium, sodium and potassium with water and represent the reactions using balanced chemical equations.

☑ Describe and explain the trend in the reactivities of Group 7 elements.

☑ Demonstrate experimentally the trend in the reactivities between chlorine, bromine and iodine using displacement reactions.

☑ Define acids and alkalis in terms of protons.

☑ Understand why hydrogen chloride is acidic in water but not in methylbenzene.

✓ UNDERSTAND

GROUP 1: THE ALKALI METALS

Some of the trends of this group are shown on the right. The trend to note is the fact that **reactivity increases downwards**.

This is because as you go down the groups, the number of electron shells increase such that the electrostatic attractions between the nucleus and the valence (outermost) electron decrease. This means it gets easier to lose the valence electron as you go down the group. We say that there is increased **shielding**: the more inner shells you have the greater shield they create on the outer electron form the positively charged nucleus.

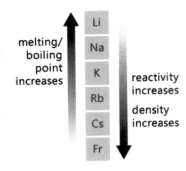

The similarity in the products and observations of the reactions between Li, Na and K with water provide a basis for their recognition as a family of elements.

REACTIONS OF LITHIUM, SODIUM AND POTASSIUM WITH WATER

Li, Na and K react with water to produce a metal hydroxide and hydrogen:

metal + water → metal hydroxide + hydrogen

All the hydroxides are **bases**, and when dissolved in water, they form an **alkaline solution**. Thus, they turn **red litmus paper blue**. Observations:

- **Lithium** floats, fizzing steadily (**effervescence**) and becomes smaller and smaller until all of it has reacted.

$$2Li(s) + 2H_2O(l) \rightarrow 2LiOH(aq) + H_2(g)$$

- **Sodium** also floats because it is less dense than water. It might melt into a ball (due to lots of heat being produced by the reaction), and move around the surface. Lots of effervescence again (due to H_2 gas evolving), and when lit, it produces a **yellow/orange flame**.

$$2Na(s) + 2H_2O(l) \rightarrow 2NaOH(aq) + H_2(g)$$

- **Potassium** reacts very quickly, and enough heat is produced to ignite the hydrogen product, which burns with a **lilac flame**. It also produces a lot of effervescence and spits around the surface of the water.

$$2K(s) + 2H_2O(l) \rightarrow 2KOH(aq) + H_2(g)$$

GROUP 7: THE HALOGENS

Halogens exist as **diatomic molecules** (i.e. pairs). Their melting/boiling points increase down the group, hence, at room temperature...

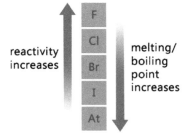

- **Chlorine** is a pale green gas
- **Bromine** is a red liquid

- **Iodine** is a grey solid

Reactivity increases up the group because as the number of electron shells decreases, the electrostatic attractions of the outermost electrons to the nucleus is stronger, increasing the likelihood of attracting electrons from other atoms to fill its outer shell.

We can show this by reacting aqueous solutions of Cl_2, Br_2 and I_2 with each of KCl, KBr and KI (potassium halides).

Observations	Potassium Chloride	Potassium Bromide	Potassium Iodide
Chlorine		colourless to orange	colourless to brown
Bromine	stays orange		orange to dark brown
Iodine	stays brown	stays brown	

The colour changes are due to the halogen in the potassium halide being displaced by a more reactive halogen. For example, the colour change from colourless to orange when $Cl_2(aq)$ reacted with KBr(aq) was due to the fact that the Br_2 was displaced. It was the colour of the bromine produced that turned the solution orange.

$$Cl_2(aq) + 2KBr(aq) \rightarrow 2KCl(aq) + Br_2(aq)$$

Notice that potassium does not change. In these reactions, it acts as a **spectator ion**. These reactions are known as **redox reactions**, where oxidation and reduction are both occurring. The ionic equations below illustrate this in the reaction between Cl_2 and KBr:

$Cl_2(aq) + 2e^- \rightarrow 2Cl^-(aq)$ chlorine is reduced, forming Cl^- ions

$2Br^-(aq) \rightarrow Br_2(aq) + 2e^-$ Br^- ions are oxidised, forming bromine

HYDROGEN CHLORIDE AND HYDROCHLORIC ACID?

Both have the chemical formula HCl, so why do they have different names? Basically hydrochloric acid is hydrogen chloride in aqueous solution, but only the former can be considered an acid.

To understand why, we have to look at **Brønsted-Lowry acid-base theory** which states that:

---

acids donate protons, bases accept protons

In aqueous solution, the hydrogen chloride dissociates (or 'splits'), giving off H^+ ions:

$$HCl(aq) \rightarrow H^+(aq) + Cl^-(aq)$$

H^+ ions are basically protons. Think about it: an H atom has 1 electron and 1 proton, but when it loses the electron to become an H^+ ion, it only consists of 1 proton.

Because of this, the HCl(aq) is 'donating protons', thus it is by definition, an acid (hydrochloric acid), whereas HCl(g) (hydrogen chloride gas) is not.

HCl IS ACIDIC IN WATER BUT NOT METHYLBENZENE?

HCl is acidic in water because when dissolved, it dissociates to give H^+ ions. This is because water is **polar** - the bonding pairs of electrons in the two O-H covalent bonds do not distribute equally around the H_2O molecule. They are pulled (for reasons beyond IGCSE) towards the O. This makes the 'O side' of the H_2O slightly negatively charged, and the 'H sides' more positively charged.

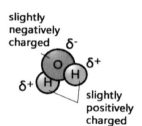

slightly negatively charged

slightly positively charged

OUR TIP

Key points to mention are that water is polar and methylbenzene isn't, so HCl will only dissociate to form H^+ ions in water. The rest here is just for explaining the theory.

This property means that the O of H_2O will become attracted towards the H of HCl, and the H of the H_2O towards the Cl of the HCl.

Thus, water molecules 'pull' HCl apart into H^+ and Cl^- ions, hence the acidity.

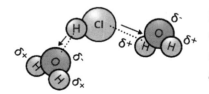

Methylbenzene isn't polar, therefore HCl does not dissociate when dissolved in it. As a result, H^+ ions are not formed, and so the solution is not considered acidic.

✓ LEARN

1. State two observations when a piece of sodium is placed in a trough of water other than that it floats. [2]

    ✓ **There will be effervescence.**
    ✓ **The sodium melts into a ball and will skim across the surface of the water.**

2. Identify the ion responsible for making a substance:

    a) Acidic [1]

    ✓ **H^+**

    b) Alkaline [1]

    ✓ **OH^-**

3. Hydrogen bromide is formed in the following reaction:

$$Br_2(g) + H_2(g) \rightarrow 2HBr(g)$$

It has similar chemical properties to hydrogen chloride. Hence, state the colour change of blue litmus paper when it is added to a *solution* of HBr. Give a reason for your answer. [2]

    ✓ **Colour change: blue to red.**
    ✓ **Reason: the hydrogen bromide solution is acidic (because the H^+ ions and the Br^- ions fully dissociate in water).**

4. A sample of hydrogen bromide is dissolved in methylbenzene. State, with a reason, the final colour of the blue litmus paper when it has been added. [2]

    ✓ **Colour: Blue**
    ✓ **Reason: The HBr does not dissociate in methylbenzene, so no H^+ ions are formed, hence the pH of the solution remains unchanged.**

5. State [and explain]* the trend in reactivity of Group 1 metals. [4]

    ✓ **Reactivity increases down the group.**
    ✓ **This is because the number of electron shells increase down the group, increasing the distance between the nucleus and the outer shell electron.***
    ✓ **This means the electrostatic attractions between the nucleus and the outer shell electron decreases down the group.***
    ✓ **Thus, it is easier to lose the outer shell electron down the group.***

6. State the colour and appearance of Cl_2, Br_2 and I_2 at room temperature. [3]

    ✓ **Cl_2 – pale green gas**
    ✓ **Br_2 – red liquid**
    ✓ **I_2 – grey solid**

7. What is observed (if any) when $Cl_2(aq)$ is added to $KBr(aq)$? If a reaction occurs, write a balanced chemical equation for it (include state symbols). [2]

    ✓ **Solution turns from colourless to orange.**
    ✓ **$Cl_2(aq) + 2KBr(aq) \rightarrow 2KCl(aq) + Br_2(aq)$**

8. Write the balanced equation for the reaction between potassium and water. [1]

    ✓ **$2K + 2H_2O \rightarrow 2KOH + H_2$**

2.3: OXYGEN & OXIDES

Here, we will be learning to:

☑ Recall the approximate percentage by volume of nitrogen, oxygen, carbon dioxide and argon in air.

☑ Demonstrate experimentally that oxygen occupies around 21% by volume of air using copper, iron and phosphorus.

☑ Describe the reactions of magnesium, sulfur and carbon with oxygen.

☑ Describe the acid-base characters of metal and non-metal oxides in solution.

☑ Prepare oxygen and carbon dioxide in the lab.

☑ Know that carbon dioxide is a greenhouse gas.

☑ Explain the properties that make carbon dioxide suitable for use in carbonated drinks and fire extinguishers.

☑ Describe the thermal decomposition of metal carbonates.

✓ UNDERSTAND

OXYGEN AND THE AIR

The table to the right shows the composition of dry air - learn it!

There are many ways in which we can show that O_2 makes up around 21% of the air.

Element	Percentage (%)
N_2	78
O_2	21
Ar	0.90
CO_2	0.04
Others	0.06

We can use **copper** for example. The initial volume of air within the apparatus shown below is measured. The syringes are pushed forwards and backwards, squeezing air over the heated copper, which turns black as copper(II) oxide is formed.

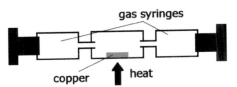

gas syringes

copper   heat

After cooling, the final volume of air is measured – around 21% should have been used up because the copper reacts with the oxygen in the air, but not with any of its other constituent parts. Therefore, the air contains 21% oxygen.

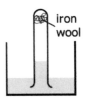

We can also use the **rusting of iron** (which involves iron reacting with oxygen to form iron(III) oxide). Damp iron wool or filings are placed inside a test tube which is inverted in a beaker of water, with the initial level of the water in the tube marked. The water level will rise up the tube as O_2 is reacted. The new level is marked. The % change in volume of water in the tube is calculated and should give ~21%.

And finally, we can also use **phosphorus**. A sample is placed on an evaporating dish which is then floated on water, with the initial water level marked. The evaporating dish is covered with a bell jar. The sample is touched with a hot rod to start the reaction between phosphorus and O_2. By the end, the O_2 will be used up, which will lower pressure in the jar, causing water to rise within the jar. The volume of water should rise by around 21% higher in the jar.

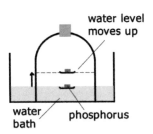

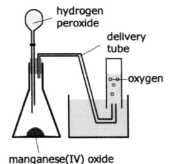

Oxygen is made in the lab from hydrogen peroxide solution using **manganese(IV) oxide** as a catalyst:

$$2H_2O_2(aq) \rightarrow 2H_2O(l) + O_2(g)$$

The O_2 given off is collected over water.

REACTIONS OF MAGNESIUM, SULFUR AND CARBON WITH OXYGEN...

Magnesium	• Produces white, powdery magnesium oxide. • Bright white flame during the reaction. • It is a basic oxide.	$2Mg(s) + O_2(g) \rightarrow 2MgO(s)$
Sulfur	• Tiny blue flame produced during the reaction. • Poisonous, colourless sulfur dioxide is produced. • It is an acidic oxide.	$S(s) + O_2(g) \rightarrow SO_2(g)$
Carbon	• Gives colourless carbon dioxide. • A small yellow-orange flame might be produced. • It is a (slightly) acidic oxide.	$C(s) + O_2(g) \rightarrow CO_2(g)$

Indeed, not only can metals and non-metals be classified on the basis of their conductivity, but the above reactions demonstrate how they can be classified on the basis of the acid-base behaviour of their oxides. **Metal oxides tend to be basic in solution**, whereas **non-metal oxides tend to be acidic in solution**. For example:

Metal oxide $CaO + H_2O \rightarrow Ca(OH)_2 \rightarrow Ca^{2+} + 2OH^-$

Non-metal oxide $CO_2 + H_2O \rightarrow H_2CO_3 \rightarrow CO_3^{2-} + 2H^+$

As you can see in the equations above, calcium oxide forms calcium hydroxide, which dissociates to form calcium and hydroxide ions (the latter of which gives metal oxides its basic properties in solution). On the other hand, carbon dioxide forms carbonic acid, which dissociates to form carbonate and hydrogen ions (the latter of which gives non-metal oxides its acidic properties in solution).

CARBON DIOXIDE

Carbon dioxide can be easily made in the lab by reacting hydrochloric acid with calcium carbonate because of the following reaction:

metal carbonate + acid → metal salt + carbon dioxide + water

The CO_2 can be collected via **downward delivery** because it is denser than air.

Its equation

$$CaCO_3(s) + 2HCl(aq) \rightarrow CaCl_2(aq) + H_2O(l) + CO_2(g)$$

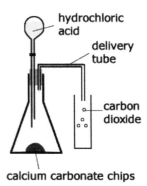

CO_2 is a **greenhouse gas** and might contribute to **global warming** by enhancing the **greenhouse effect**. This basically increases the amount of **long-wave infrared radiation** (entering the atmosphere from the Sun) that gets reflected back to the Earth, thus heating up the Earth.

Some properties of carbon dioxide:

- Colourless and odourless gas.
- **Slightly soluble in water** but more so under pressure, thus, is used in **carbonated drinks**. When bottle is opened, pressure falls and gas bubbles out of the solution.
- Denser than air - hence, is used in **fire extinguishers** as carbon dioxide 'sinks' onto the flames and prevents any more oxygen from reaching them.

Metal carbonates can also be thermally decomposed (i.e. broken down into their constituent parts over heat):

metal carbonate $\xrightarrow{\Delta}$ metal oxide + carbon dioxide
(The 'Δ' just means on heating).

✓ LEARN

1. Are metal oxides basic or acidic? [1]

   ✓ **Metal oxides are basic.**

2. Are non-metal oxides basic or acidic? [1]

   ✓ **Non-metal oxides are acidic.**

3. Give two industrial uses of carbon dioxide. [2]

   ✓ **Fire extinguishers**
   ✓ **Fizzy drinks**

4. Write the balanced equation for the decomposition of hydrogen peroxide. [1]

   ✓ $\mathbf{2H_2O_2 \rightarrow 2H_2O + O_2}$

5. Write the balanced equation for the reaction used to prepare carbon dioxide gas in the lab (include state symbols). Explain why collection by downward delivery is possible. [2]

   ✓ $\mathbf{CaCO_3(s) + 2HCl(aq) \rightarrow CaCl_2(aq) + H_2O(l) + CO_2(g)}$
   ✓ **Carbon dioxide gas is denser than air.**

6. On average, what % of air is made up of: **a)** N_2; **b)** O_2; **c)** CO_2; and **d)** argon? [4]

   ✓ **a) 78%**
   ✓ **b) 21%**
   ✓ **c) 0.04%**
   ✓ **d) 0.90%**

2.4: HYDROGEN & WATER

Here, we will be learning to:

☑ Describe the reactions of magnesium, aluminium, zinc and iron with dilute hydrochloric acid and dilute sulfuric acids.

☑ Recall that water is produced by the combustion of hydrogen.

☑ Describe chemical tests to show the presence of water.

☑ Describe how the purity of water can be tested.

✓ UNDERSTAND

Metals above hydrogen on the reactivity series (more on this later) will react with an acid to form a salt and hydrogen:

---

metal + acid → salt + hydrogen

REACTIONS WITH DILUTE $HCl(aq)$ AND $H_2SO_4(aq)$

Magnesium reacts vigorously with cold dilute acids. There will be lots of effervescence and a colourless solution will be formed. The reaction is also **exothermic**, meaning it produces lots of heat.

$$Mg(s) + 2HCl(aq) \rightarrow MgCl_2(aq) + H_2(g)$$
$$Mg(s) + H_2SO_4(aq) \rightarrow MgSO_4(aq) + H_2(g)$$

Aluminium starts off reacting slowly, but reacts more vigorously if warmed. This is because aluminium is **covered with a layer of aluminium oxide**, which stops the acid reaching the aluminium underneath. Heating allows the acid to remove this layer more quickly.

$$2Al(s) + 6HCl(aq) \rightarrow 2AlCl_3(aq) + 3H_2(g)$$
$$2Al(s) + 3H_2SO_4(aq) \rightarrow Al_2(SO_4)_3(aq) + 3H_2(g)$$

Iron and **zinc** both react very slowly when cold (though zinc reacts quicker). However, they react more rapidly on heating. Some effervescence will be produced. The aqueous solutions of iron(II) salts produced are pale green.

$$Zn(s) + 2HCl(aq) \rightarrow ZnCl_2(aq) + H_2(g)$$
$$Zn(s) + H_2SO_4(aq) \rightarrow ZnSO_4(aq) + H_2(g)$$

$$Fe(s) + 2HCl(aq) \rightarrow FeCl_2(aq) + H_2(g)$$
$$Fe(s) + H_2SO_4(aq) \rightarrow FeSO_4(aq) + H_2(g)$$

ALL ABOUT WATER

Water is formed from the combustion of hydrogen:

$$2H_2(g) + O_2(g) \rightarrow 2H_2O(l)$$

The reaction occurs when both reactants are in the presence of a flame. It gives a **squeaky 'pop' sound** (and this reaction forms the basis of the test for H_2 gas) and the reaction is violent - possibly explosive. It also produces lots of heat.

A **chemical test** for water involves using **anhydrous copper(II) sulfate** (i.e. 'dehydrated' or 'dry' copper(II) sulfate). Water hydrates this powder, turning it from **white to blue**.

adding water hydrates the copper(II) sulphate

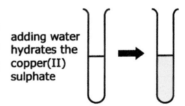

Another test involves using **blue cobalt(II) chloride paper**, which turns from **blue to pink** in the presence of water.

Tests for water:	anhydrous copper(II) sulfate	white → blue
	blue cobalt(II) chloride paper	blue → pink

Water is **pure** if it freezes at exactly 0°C and boils at 100°C. If it boils over a range of temperatures, it is impure.

✓ LEARN

1. What substance can be used as a chemical test for the presence of water and what colour change is seen when water is present? [1]

   ✓ **EITHER: Anhydrous copper (II) sulfate turns from white to blue when water is present.**
   ✓ **OR: cobalt(II) chloride paper turns from blue to pink when water is present.**

2. Write the balanced chemical equation for the combustion of hydrogen, with state symbols. [1]

   ✓ $2H_2(g) + O_2(g) \rightarrow 2H_2O(l)$

3. Write the balanced chemical equations for the reactions of magnesium, aluminium and zinc with hydrochloric acid. Include state symbols. [3]

   ✓ $Mg(s) + 2HCl(aq) \rightarrow MgCl_2(aq) + H_2(g)$
   ✓ $2Al(s) + 6HCl(aq) \rightarrow 2AlCl_3(aq) + 3H_2(g)$
   ✓ $Zn(s) + 2HCl(aq) \rightarrow ZnCl_2(aq) + H_2(g)$

4. Write the balanced chemical equations for the reactions of magnesium, aluminium and iron with sulfuric acid. Include state symbols. [3]

   ✓ $Mg(s) + H_2SO_4(aq) \rightarrow MgSO_4(aq) + H_2(g)$
   ✓ $2Al(s) + 3H_2SO_4(aq) \rightarrow Al_2(SO_4)_3(aq) + 3H_2(g)$
   ✓ $Fe(s) + H_2SO_4(aq) \rightarrow FeSO_4(aq) + H_2(g)$

5. Why is the reaction between aluminium and hydrochloric acid initially slow? [1]

   ✓ **Al is covered by a layer of Al_2O_3 which prevents the acid reaching the Al.**

2.5: THE REACTIVITY SERIES

Here, we will be learning to:

☑ Recall the positions of potassium, sodium, lithium, calcium, magnesium, aluminium, carbon, zinc, iron, hydrogen, copper, silver and gold in the reactivity series.

☑ Describe ways to deduce the position of metals in the reactivity series.

☑ Define oxidation and reduction in terms of oxygen.

☑ Define redox, oxidising agent and reducing agent.

☑ Recall that water and oxygen must be present for iron to rust.

☑ Describe ways to prevent iron from rusting.

✓ UNDERSTAND

DISPLACEMENT REACTIONS

We met **displacement reactions** earlier with a more reactive halogen displacing a less reactive halide.

> **OUR TIP**
>
> Remember this mnemonic: **p**retty **S**ally **L**annister **c**ould **m**arry **a** **C**hristian **Z**ulu **i**n **l**ovely **H**onolulu **c**atching **s**ome **g**eese.

potassium
sodium
lithium
calcium
magnesium
aluminium
carbon
zinc
iron
hydrogen
copper
silver
gold

reactivity

Elements can be placed according to their reactivity in the **reactivity series** - you have to learn those shown to the left.

If a metal is above another in the reactivity series, it can displace the other metal. For example:

$$3ZnO(s) + 2Al(s) \rightarrow Al_2O_3(s) + 3Zn(s)$$

Examiners love this section - make sure you understand it!

DEDUCING THE REACTIVITY SERIES

There are many ways to deduce the order of reactivity series:

- **Reacting metals with other metal salts in aqueous solution:** if a reaction occurs, the metal introduced into the solution must have displaced the metal that was originally in solution from its salt. This shows that the metal introduced is higher in the reactivity series than the other metal that has now been displaced. An example:

$$CuSO_4(aq) + Fe(s) \rightarrow FeSO_4(aq) + Cu(s)$$

In the above, one would observe the blue of the copper(II) sulfate solution disappearing, eventually resulting in a pale green solution of iron(II) sulfate.

- **Reacting metals with dilute acids:** we would expect metals potassium → magnesium to react more vigorously and quickly than zinc and iron. In fact, it is probably not safe to put Group 1 metals into acids unless the acid is very, very dilute. We would also expect copper not to react because it is lower than hydrogen in reactivity series.

- **Reacting metals with water:** K, Na and Li would react vigorously to produce H_2 gas and their respective metal hydroxides. Ca would produce the same products but would react slower. Mg → Fe would react with steam to produce their respective oxides and H_2 gas. Copper would not react.

Displacement reactions are **redox reactions** - both oxidation and reduction occur. We mentioned this earlier, but now we will introduce two more terms:

- An **oxidising agent** is an e^- acceptor (it oxidises something else, thus getting reduced in the processes).
- A **reducing agent** is an e^- donor (it reduces something else, thus getting oxidised in the process).

So in the equation given above:

$$CuSO_4(aq) + Fe(s) \rightarrow FeSO_4(aq) + Cu(s)$$

Fe is the reducing agent (donates e⁻):　　　$Fe(s) \rightarrow Fe^{2+}(aq) + 2e^-$
Cu²⁺ is the oxidising agent (accepts e⁻):　　$Cu^{2+}(aq) + 2e^- \rightarrow Cu(s)$

SO_4^{2-} is just the **spectator ion** here.

RUSTING

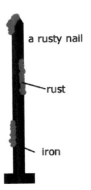

a rusty nail

rust

iron

Iron will rust in the presence of **oxygen** and **water**. It oxidises to form **hydrated iron(III) oxide**, which is **red-brown**.

We can understand oxidation/reduction not just in terms of electrons, but also in terms of oxygen:

---

oxidation is the addition of oxygen and reduction is the removal of oxygen

---

Rusting of iron can be prevented by:

- **Grease/oil/paint/plastic** – used to cover iron, creating a barrier so that the oxygen and water are not in direct contact with the iron.
- **Galvanising** – coating iron with a thin layer of zinc, a more reactive metal than iron itself. Since zinc is higher in the reactivity series than iron, it will react with oxygen and water instead of iron, preventing rusting.
- **Sacrificial protection** – similar to galvanising, except instead of coating iron with a more reactive metal, a large block (**the sacrificial anode**) is connected to the iron. If the iron rusts (i.e. becomes oxidised), the anode will provide electrons to reduce it.
- **Alloying** - mixing iron with another metal to give it anti-rusting properties (e.g. mixing it with steel).

✓ LEARN

1. What is the chemical name for rust? What colour is it? [2]

    ✓ **Iron (III) oxide**
    ✓ **Red/brown**

2. What two substances must be present for iron to rust? [2]

    ✓ **Water**
    ✓ **Oxygen (allow 'air')**

3. State three ways in which one can prevent iron from rusting. [3]

    Any 3 of:
    ✓ **Covering with paint/oil/grease/plastic.**
    ✓ **Galvanising**
    ✓ **Sacrificial protection**
    ✓ **Alloying**

4. If I try to react copper with dilute sulfuric acid, what will I observe? [1]

    ✓ **No visible change**

5. Write the balanced chemical equation for the reaction that occurs (if any) after I place magnesium in a solution of iron(II) sulfate. Include state symbols. [1]

    ✓ $FeSO_4(aq) + Mg(s) \rightarrow MgSO_4(aq) + Fe(s)$

6. From Q5, which is the oxidising agent and which is the reducing agent? [2]

    ✓ **Iron(II)/Fe^{2+} is the oxidising agent.**
    ✓ **Magnesium is the reducing agent.**

2.6: TESTS FOR IONS + GASES

Here, we will be learning to:

☑ Use flame tests to test for the presence of Li^+, Na^+, K^+, Ca^{2+} ions.

☑ Use sodium hydroxide solution to test for the presence of NH_4^+, Cu^{2+}, Fe^{2+} and Fe^{3+} ions.

☑ Use nitric acid and silver nitric solution to test for the presence of Cl^-, Br^- and I^- ions.

☑ Use hydrochloric acid and barium chloride solution to test for the presence of SO_4^{2-} ions.

☑ Use an acid to test for the presence of CO_3^{2-} ions.

☑ Test for hydrogen, oxygen, carbon dioxide, ammonia and chlorine.

✓ UNDERSTAND
∙∙

FLAME TESTS - Li^+, Na^+, K^+ AND Ca^{2+}

The following steps are used to carry out a flame test:

1. Dip a **nichrome wire** in acid, and then in a Bunsen burner flame (**blue flame must be used**). This removes impurities on the wire.
2. Dip the wire in acid again, and then into a sample of the metal/metal ion and place it in the flame.

Metal Cation	Colour
Lithium ion Li^+	Crimson Red
Sodium ion Na^+	Yellow/Orange
Potassium ion K^+	Lilac
Calcium ion Ca^{2+}	Brick Red

ADDING SODIUM HYDROXIDE SOLUTION - NH_4^+, Cu^{2+}, Fe^{2+} AND Fe^{3+}

Reacting Cu^{2+}, Fe^{2+} or Fe^{3+} ions with NaOH(aq) will lead to the formation of insoluble hydroxides which will **precipitate** out of the solution.

Metal Cation	Colour of Precipitate	Ionic Equation
Copper ion Cu^{2+}	Blue	$Cu^{2+}(aq) + 2OH^-(aq) \rightarrow Cu(OH)_2(s)$
Iron ion Fe^{2+}	Green	$Fe^{2+}(aq) + 2OH^-(aq) \rightarrow Fe(OH)_2(s)$
Iron ion Fe^{3+}	Brown	$Fe^{3+}(aq) + 3OH^-(aq) \rightarrow Fe(OH)_3(s)$

Reacting NH_4^+ ions with $NaOH(aq)$ will lead to the formation of ammonium hydroxide NH_4OH, a colourless solution. When the solution is heated, ammonia gas will be given off which turns **red litmus paper blue**.

$$NH_4^+(aq) + OH^-(aq) \rightarrow NH_3(g) + H_2O(l)$$

ADDING ACIDIFIED SILVER NITRATE SOLUTION - Cl^-, Br^-, AND I^-

1. Add a few drops of **dilute nitric acid** to an aqueous solution of the solid being tested. This prevents the formation of other insoluble silver compounds. You cannot use $HCl(aq)$ because it contains chloride ions.
2. Add **silver nitrate solution** and look for a precipitate. These will be silver chloride, silver bromide or silver iodide.

Halide Ion	Colour of Precipitate	Ionic Equation
Chloride ion Cl^-	White	$Ag^+(aq) + Cl^-(aq) \rightarrow AgCl(s)$
Bromide ion Br^-	Pale Cream	$Ag^+(aq) + Br^-(aq) \rightarrow AgBr(s)$
Iodide ion I^-	Yellow	$Ag^+(aq) + I^-(aq) \rightarrow AgI(s)$

ADDING ACIDIFIED BARIUM CHLORIDE SOLUTION – SO_4^{2-}

1. Add a few drops of **dilute hydrochloric acid** to an aqueous solution of the solid being tested - this removes SO_3^{2-} sulphite ions which can give the same result (a white precipitate) as sulfates.
2. Add **barium chloride solution** - a **white precipitate** of the insoluble barium sulfate will form in the presence of SO_4^{2-} ions.

$$Ba^{2+}(aq) + SO_4^{2-}(aq) \rightarrow BaSO_4(s)$$

ADDING DILUTE HYDROCHLORIC ACID OR NITRIC ACID – CO_3^{2-}

To test for carbonates, simply add some dilute acid to the solid, or an aqueous solution of the solid, being tested because...

> **metal carbonate + acid → metal salt + carbon dioxide + water**

All we need to do is add some dilute hydrochloric acid or nitric acid, and confirm that the gas that is given off is CO_2.

We can do this by bubbling it through **limewater** (calcium hydroxide solution) which turns from **colourless to cloudy/milky white**:

$$CO_3^{2-}(aq) + 2H^+(aq) \rightarrow CO_2(g) + H_2O(l)$$
$$Ca(OH)_2(aq) + CO_2(g) \rightarrow CaCO_3(s) + H_2O(l)$$

> ## GOLDEN RULE
> **ALWAYS STATE THE INITIAL COLOUR AND THE FINAL COLOUR OF THE SOLUTION OR PRECIPITATE IF THERE IS A COLOUR CHANGE.**

TESTING FOR GASES

Gas	Test
H_2	A lighted wooden splint makes a popping sound in a test tube of hydrogen.
O_2	A glowing wooden splint relights in a test tube of oxygen.
CO_2	Bubble the test gas through limewater - turns from colourless to cloudy/milky white.
NH_3	It turns damp red litmus paper blue (and has a characteristic pungent smell).
Cl_2	It makes damp blue litmus paper turn red, and then bleaches it white (and has a characteristic sharp, choking smell).

✓ LEARN

1. Fill this table for observations using the flame test: [4]

Metal Ion	Colour
K^+	
Ca^{2+}	
Li^+	
Na^+	

    ✓ **(From top to bottom): lilac, brick red, crimson red, yellow/orange.**

2. Describe how you would test for sulfate ions in a sample of sodium sulfate solution. Write a balanced chemical equation for the reaction. Include state symbols. [4]

    ✓ **Add a few drops of HCl(aq).**
    ✓ **Add BaCl$_2$ solution.**
    ✓ **White precipitate forms from colourless solution if SO_4^{2-} present.**
    ✓ **$Na_2SO_4(aq) + BaCl_2(aq) \rightarrow 2NaCl(aq) + BaSO_4(s)$.**

3. When testing for halide ions, why do we need to add a few drops of nitric acid first? What step(s) do we take after? [2]

    ✓ **Prevents formation of other insoluble silver compounds.**
    ✓ **Add silver nitrate solution, and look at the colour of the precipitate formed.**

4. If we used the procedure from the answers to Q3, what will we observe for Cl^-, Br^- and I^- ions from the colourless solution? [3]

    ✓ **White precipitate**
    ✓ **Pale cream precipitate**
    ✓ **Yellow precipitate**

5. How would I show that ammonium ions were present in a solution? [3]

   ✓ **Add NaOH(aq).**
   ✓ **Heat gently.**
   ✓ **Test for ammonia gas - it will turn damp red litmus paper blue.**

6. What happens if I place damp blue litmus paper in chlorine gas? [1]

   ✓ **It turns red, and then bleaches white.**

7. I bubble CO_2 through limewater. Write the balanced chemical equation for the reaction that occurs (with state symbols) and state what is observed and why. [3]

   ✓ **$Ca(OH)_2(aq) + CO_2(g) \rightarrow CaCO_3(s) + H_2O(l)$**
   ✓ **Turns from colourless to cloudy/milky white...**
   ✓ **Due to the $CaCO_3$ precipitate.**

8. I put sodium into a beaker of water. There is lots of effervescence. I place a lighted wooden split near the gas. State what I observe and write the equation for the reaction that produces the observation. [2]

   ✓ **A 'pop' sound**
   ✓ **$2H_2 + O_2 \rightarrow 2H_2O$**

9. How do you test for O_2 gas? [1]

   ✓ **A glowing wooden splint relights in the presence of oxygen.**

2.7: ACIDS, ALKALIS, SALTS...

Here, we will be learning to:

☑ Recall that acids are sources of H^+ ions and alkalis are sources of OH^- ions.

☑ Describe the results of litmus paper, methyl orange and phenolphthalein in both acidic and alkaline solutions.

☑ Understand the use of the pH scale and how universal indicator can be used to measure the pH of a solution.

☑ Predict the products of reactions between metals, metal oxides and metal carbonates with hydrochloric, sulfuric and nitric acids, and write balanced equations for such.

☑ Learn the solubility rules of common salts in water and use these rules to select suitable reagents to prepare both insoluble and soluble salts.

✓ UNDERSTAND

We already know (hopefully) at this stage that:

- **Acids** are sources of H^+ ions.
- **Alkalis** are sources of OH^- ions.

There are many indicators to distinguish between the two, for example:

	Acid	Alkali
Litmus		
Methyl Orange		
Phenolphthalein		

- **Litmus paper:** acids turn blue litmus paper red; alkalis turn red litmus paper blue.
- **Methyl orange:** red in acids; yellow in alkalis.
- **Phenolphthalein:** colourless in acids; pink in alkalis.

How strongly acidic a substance is, can be determined on a pH scale, which is a measure of the concentration of H^+ ions. The pH scale ranges from 0-14:

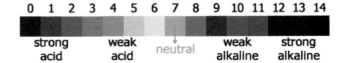

| 0 | 1 | 2 | 3 | 4 | 5 | 6 | 7 | 8 | 9 | 10 | 11 | 12 | 13 | 14 |

strong acid   weak acid   neutral   weak alkaline   strong alkaline

Universal indicator can be used to measure the **approximate pH** of a solution because it gives a wide range of colours each associated with a pH value.

We can predict the products when metals, metal oxides and metal carbonates react with acids - some of which we've already come across:

> **acid + metal → metal salt + hydrogen**
> **acid + metal oxide → metal salt + water**
> **acid + metal carbonate → metal salt + carbon dioxide + water**

By metal salts, we mean that:

- Reactions with hydrochloric acid form metal chlorides.
- Reactions with sulfuric acid form metal sulfates.
- Reactions with nitric acid form metal nitrates (you don't need to learn what happens between a metal itself and nitric acid).

PRECIPITATION REACTIONS

There are some general rules for predicting solubility in water:

- All common Na^+, K^+ and NH_4^+ salts are soluble.
- All nitrates are soluble.
- Common chlorides are soluble, except silver chloride.
- Common sulfates are soluble, except those of barium and calcium.
- Common carbonates are insoluble, except those of Na^+, K^+ and NH_4^+.

Precipitation reactions produce a precipitate, an insoluble solid that emerges from a reaction taking place in aqueous solution (e.g. between two metal salts in solution).

So, let's try preparing silver chloride. We will need a soluble chloride and a soluble silver salt. We know that all nitrates are soluble, and that Na, K and NH_4^+ salts are soluble so let's try...

OUR TIP

If, for whatever reason you end up producing more than one solid product, you might need to change your reagents!

$$AgNO_3(aq) + NaCl(aq) \rightarrow AgCl(s) + NaNO_3(aq)$$

The silver chloride can be filtered, washed with water and dried between two pieces of filter paper.

What about preparing soluble salts such as those of sodium, potassium and ammonium? We will need to use **titration**, which involves adding JUST enough of reagent 1 to reagent 2 so everything reacts. This is so only the soluble salts made are found in solution, not any excess reagent.

1. Use a solution of metal hydroxide (e.g. KOH) and an acid (e.g. sulfuric acid).
2. Pipette 25 cm^3 of the acid solution into a conical flask.
3. Add a few drops of phenolphthalein or methyl orange indicator.
4. Add hydroxide from the burette until the **end point** of the titration is reached (i.e. indicated when one drop changes the indicator's colour in the whole solution). When doing so, record the volume of hydroxide added.
5. Repeat the above steps, without the indicator, using the same amount of acid and alkali as recorded in the first titration.
6. Transfer the contents of the conical flask into an evaporating basin. Evaporate some of the solution. Then leave to crystalise.
7. Filter and dry between two pieces of filter paper.

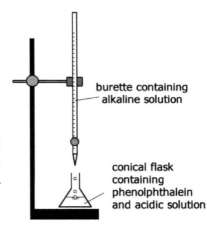

burette containing alkaline solution

conical flask containing phenolphthalein and acidic solution

But which acid do we pick to neutralise the hydroxide? In general:

- **Hydrochloric acid** leads to the formation of metal chlorides.
- **Sulfuric acid** leads to the formation of metal sulfates.
- **Nitric acid** leads to the formation of metal nitrates.

Furthermore, we do not necessarily have to neutralise a metal hydroxide. We can neutralise metals, metal oxides and metal carbonates as well to make our desired salt. For example, if I want to make K_2SO_4, I can do so using a variety of combinations of reagents:

Potassium hydroxide and sulfuric acid: $2KOH + H_2SO_4 \rightarrow K_2SO_4 + 2H_2O$

Potassium and sulfuric acid: $2K + H_2SO_4 \rightarrow K_2SO_4 + H_2$

Potassium oxide and sulfuric acid: $K_2O + H_2SO_4 \rightarrow K_2SO_4 + H_2O$

Potassium carbonate and sulfuric acid: $K_2CO_3 + H_2SO_4 \rightarrow K_2SO_4 + H_2O + CO_2$

✓ **LEARN**

1. What colour does universal indicator turn in:

   a) A strong acid? [1]

      ✓ **Red**

   b) A weak acid? [1]

      ✓ **Yellow**

   c) A neutral substance? [1]

      ✓ **Green**

   d) A weak alkali? [1]

      ✓ **Blue**

   e) A strong alkali? [1]

      ✓ **Purple**

2. I want to make some potassium nitrate.

   a) Suggest two reagents I can use. [2]

      ✓ **Potassium hydroxide**
      ✓ **Nitric acid**

   b) What lab procedure should I use to obtain the potassium nitrate? [1]

      ✓ **Titration**

3. I want to make some calcium sulfate.

    a) Suggest two reagents I can use. [2]

        ✓ **Any soluble calcium salt (e.g. calcium nitrate)**
        ✓ **Any soluble sulfate (e.g. sodium sulfate)**

    b) Write a balanced chemical equation for the two reagents used in part a). Include state symbols. [1]

        ✓ **E.g. $Ca(NO_3)_2(aq) + Na_2SO_4(aq) \rightarrow CaSO_4(s) + 2NaNO_3(aq)$**

    c) What do we call this type of reaction? [1]

        ✓ **Precipitation reaction**

    d) How would we obtain the calcium sulfate from the rest of the products or excess reagents? [3]

        ✓ **Filter out the calcium sulfate using filter paper.**
        ✓ **Rinse the calcium sulfate with water.**
        ✓ **Dry between two pieces of filter paper.**

4. Suggest two reagents I could use to make the following:

   a) Magnesium carbonate [2]

   ✓ **Any soluble Mg salt e.g. $Mg(NO_3)_2$**
   ✓ **Any soluble carbonate e.g. Na_2CO_3**

   b) Barium sulfate [2]

   ✓ **Any soluble Ba salt e.g. $BaCl_2$**
   ✓ **And any soluble sulfate e.g. K_2SO_4**

   c) Sodium chloride [2]

   ✓ **Any basic Na compound e.g. NaOH, Na_2CO_3**
   ✓ **Hydrochloric acid**

   d) Copper carbonate [2]

   ✓ **Any soluble Cu salt e.g. $CuCl_2$**
   ✓ **Any soluble carbonate (e.g. Na_2CO_3) or carbonic acid**

   e) Potassium nitrate [2]

   ✓ **Any basic potassium compound e.g. KOH, K_2CO_3**
   ✓ **Nitric acid**

5. Identify the reagent needed to make the following:

   a) Sodium chloride from sodium metal [1]

   ✓ **Hydrochloric acid**

   b) Magnesium sulfate from magnesium oxide [1]

   ✓ **Sulfuric acid**

✓ SECTION 2: MANIPULATE

(Total: 50 marks)

These questions will require you to utilise what you know from multiple chapters of this section. Try your best!

1. What is the chemical equation for the reaction between sulfuric acid and magnesium? Include state symbols. [2]

2. Chris breaks into the chemistry storeroom and finds some zinc(II) carbonate. He decides to perform experiments on it.

   a) Give the chemical equation for the reaction when zinc(II) carbonate is heated strongly. Include state symbols. [2]
   b) Chris puts an excess of zinc(II) carbonate in hydrochloric acid. Give the chemical equation for the reaction occurs. Include state symbols. [2]
   c) He observes lots of gas being evolved. Having not revised carbonates, he decides to test what it is. He puts a glowing splint in the gas. What does he observe? [1]
   d) He also decides to bubble it through some limewater. What does he observe? [1]
   e) Again, having not revised carbonates, Chris is not sure what the colourless solution from the reaction is! How can he show with a chemical test that it contains water? [1]
   f) Finally, Chris drops some acidified silver nitrate into the colourless solution. What does he observe? [1]

3. Denis is revising reactivities.

   a) State [and explain]* the trend in reactivities of Group 1 metals. [3]
   b) State [and explain]* the trend in reactivities of Group 7 halogens. [3]
   c) Denis also breaks into the chemistry storeroom and randomly picks up two
       bottles. One is labelled 'potassium iodide' and the other is labelled 'bromine'. He
       mixes the two together. Write the chemical equation for the reaction that occurs,
       with state symbols included. [2]
   d) What is this type of reaction called? [1]

   e) Fill in the gaps in the reactivity series below: [6]

potassium

_____

lithium

_____

magnesium

_____

carbon

_____

iron
hydrogen

_____

_____

gold

4. Greg breaks into the secret room of the chemistry storeroom and finds a cupboard labelled 'Group 1 metals'. He takes some out.

    a) He uses tweezers to pick up some potassium. In the process, he accidentally drops it into a wet sink. Describe two observations that he makes. [2]
    b) Write an equation for the above reaction, with state symbols. [2]
    c) He drops some universal indicator into the sink. What colour does he expect to see? [1]
    d) Give two definitions (each) of oxidation and reduction. [4]
    e) Did potassium get oxidised or reduced? State and explain why. [2]
    f) Chris's crucible containing the zinc carbonate explodes and the Bunsen burner, still alight, is sent flying into the sink that Greg dropped potassium into. What colour does the flame of the Bunsen burner change to now it is in contact with potassium? [1]
    g) Greg turns on the tap in a futile attempt to extinguish the flames. A lot of steam is produced and travels into an opened bottle of magnesium. Write the chemical equation (plus state symbols) of the reaction that occurs in the bottle of magnesium. [2]
    h) The flame, still coming from the Bunsen burner, produces carbon dioxide. How might this contribute to climate change? [1]
    i) The smoke alarm goes off, and fireman Richard rushes in with his fire extinguisher, which does not spray water but some gas. Suggest what gas this was and why it was suitable for extinguishing the flames. [2]

5. James has a secret obsession with oxygen.

    a) What percentage of air does O_2 make up (on average)? [1]
    b) Describe one way he can show that O_2 makes up that percentage of the air. [1]
    c) James wants to increase the concentration of O_2 in the classroom, so he decides to prepare it in the lab. State the reagent(s) and catalyst, and write a balanced equation (plus state symbols) for the reaction. [4]
    d) What is the chemical formula for rust? [1]
    e) State two ways in which James can prevent the formation of rust. [2]

SECTION 3:

ORGANIC CHEMISTRY

3.1: ALKANES & ALKENES

Here, we will be learning to:

☑ Describe the features of a homologous series.

☑ Name simple hydrocarbons using the IUPAC system of nomenclature.

☑ Know that alkanes have the general formula C_nH_{2n+2} and be able to name and draw the displayed formulae for those with up to five carbon atoms.

☑ Understand the complete and incomplete combustion of alkanes.

☑ Understand the dangers of carbon monoxide.

☑ Describe the formation of bromomethane.

☑ Recall that alkenes have the general formula C_nH_{2n} and be able to name and draw the displayed formulae for those with up to four carbon atoms.

☑ Describe the use of bromine water to test for alkenes.

✓ UNDERSTAND

INTRODUCTION TO HYDROCARBONS

Organic chemistry is the study of organic substances (i.e. those containing carbon). Much of organic chemistry at IGCSE is based on **hydrocarbons** - compounds that contain **only carbon and hydrogen**.

Hydrocarbons can be split into different classes, each containing a unique **general formula** - a chemical formula showing the ratio of each element, and that all the compounds included in that class shares those same ratios. It might look something like this C_nH_{2n} - meaning that all hydrocarbons belonging to that class has a ratio of 1 carbon atom for every 2 hydrogen atoms.

Each 'class' is known as a **homologous series**, and members share many characteristics, including:

- **Similar chemical properties** - they react similarly to other members of the series.

- **Gradation in physical properties** - meaning as the compounds get bigger, their physical properties also change at a predictable rate (e.g. melting/boiling points increase as compounds get bigger).
- **Same general formula**.

Nomenclature looks at the naming of these organic compounds - many of which you'll come across might look something like this:

There is a system for naming compounds, called the IUPAC nomenclature. The prefixes for these names are based on the **number of carbons in the longest chain:**

# of carbons	prefix
1	meth
2	eth
3	prop
4	but
5	pent

For example, with the pictures above, we'd know that the compound's name on the left name begins with an 'eth', and the middle one with a 'but'.

Sometimes the carbon chain is **branched. Branched CH₃ chains have the suffix '-yl'.** With the right picture, the hydrocarbon starts with 2-methyl, it has a CH_3 branch on carbon #2 (from the left). **Branched names come first!**

side chain	means...
methyl	$CH_3 -$
ethyl	$C_2H_5 -$

So the right hydrocarbon should be something like: '2-methyl but-'. If this all seems confusing, it will all become clearer in the next section!

ALKANES

The **alkanes** are a homologous series, with a suffix ending with **'ane'**.

The general formula for alkanes: C_nH_{2n+2}

With naming, we must first:

1. Confirm that the compound is an alkane. This can be done by counting the Cs and Hs and seeing if they fit the ratio of C_nH_{2n+2}.
2. Look for, and name any other side chains.
3. Identify the longest carbon chain, and put a prefix to it (e.g. meth, eth...).
4. End it with an 'ane'.

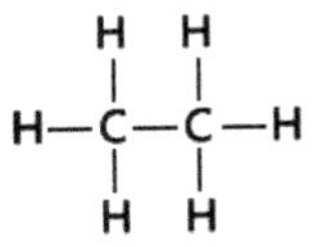

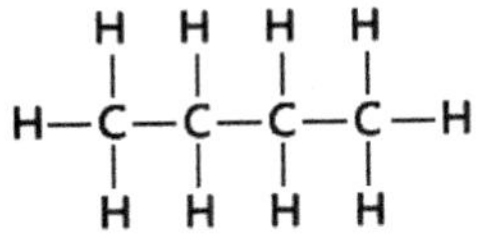

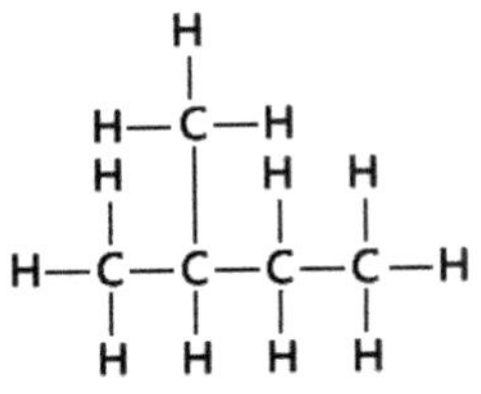

So using the same examples:

- The left hydrocarbon is called **eth**ane.
- The middle hydrocarbon is called **but**ane.
- The right hydrocarbon is called 2-methyl**but**ane.

You'll understand more once you practice the 'Learn' questions!

As hydrocarbons such as alkanes get larger, they tend to have the same chemical formula, but can be arranged differently. For example, with C_4H_{10}:

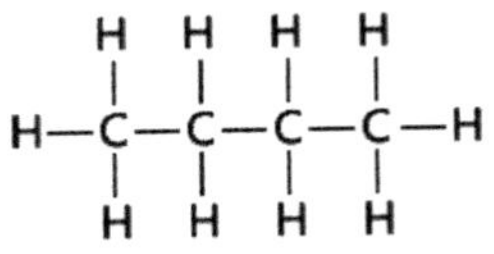

butane

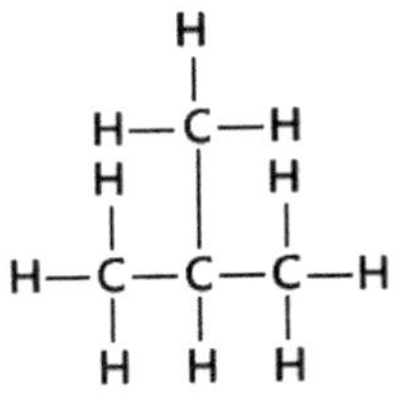

2-methylpropane

The two are examples of **isomers** - compounds with the same molecular formula but different structural formulae (i.e. they are arranged differently).

Because of this, it is preferred that you write your hydrocarbons in equations as **structural formulae** - butane would be $CH_3CH_2CH_2CH_3$, and 2-methylpropane would be $CH_3CH(CH_3)CH_3$ (the brackets enclosing the CH_3 shows that it is a chemical group that is independent of the 'main' carbon chain, thus showing it is branched).

In questions, you might be asked to draw the **displayed formula** - basically, this is where you must **show all bonds**. The pictures above are examples of this.

OUR TIP

When drawing displayed formulae, make sure each carbon only has a **maximum of 4 bonds!**

You can see that in alkanes, the carbons cannot form any more bonds, because they each form four covalent bonds, and thus, have achieved a full outer shell. We say that alkanes are **saturated hydrocarbons** - the carbon chain **only consists of single C-C bonds** and thus, each carbon atom cannot bond to anymore atoms.

Because alkanes are fuels, they can undergo **complete combustion**:

alkane + oxygen → water + carbon dioxide

For example, with methane:

$$CH_4(g) + 2O_2(g) \rightarrow 2H_2O(l) + CO_2(g)$$

However, if there is not enough oxygen, alkanes will undergo **incomplete combustion**. This can produce **carbon monoxide (CO)** - a colourless, odourless and poisonous gas. It is dangerous because it can bind to haemoglobin in our blood and stop it from carrying oxygen around the body. This can lead to death.

Alkanes react with bromine under the **presence of ultra-violet (UV) light**. One H atom from the hydrocarbon would be replaced by a Br atom, and as a result, the reaction is known as a **substitution reaction**.

$CH_4(g) + Br_2(g) \rightarrow CH_3Br(g) + HBr(g)$

ALKENES

The alkenes are another homologous series, with a suffix ending with **'ene'**.

> **The general formula for alkenes: C_nH_{2n}**

Alkenes have a C=C double bond, and as such, it is **unsaturated** - it is possible for carbon atoms involved in the double bond to form extra single bonds (if the double bond breaks).

The nomenclature process is identical to that of alkanes (except you use 'ene' instead of 'ane'). In addition, with larger alkenes, you have to specify the location of the C=C double bond.

ethene   but-1-ene   but-2-ene

Why is the alkene named but-1-ene not but-3-ene? Surely the double bond is on the 3rd carbon from the left? Well, if you flip it vertically (i.e. imagine a mirrored version), you'll realise that but-1-ene and but-3-ene are the same thing. However, it is preferred that we use the smallest possible number we can, so but-1-ene is used.

> ## GOLDEN RULE
> **WHEN STATING THE LOCATION OF THE C=C BOND OR METHYL GROUP ON THE CARBON CHAIN, USE THE SMALLEST NUMBER TO DESCRIBE IT.**

Alkenes decolourise in the presence of bromine water in what is known as an **addition reaction** (the C=C bonds break so each carbon atom can bond to a bromine atom), for example, with ethene:

$$CH_2=CH_2(g) + Br_2(aq) \rightarrow CH_2BrCH_2Br(aq)$$

The product is called **1,2-dibromoethane**. Alkanes don't react with bromine water, thus it acts as a chemical test for alkenes:

> **Alkenes turn bromine water orange to colourless.**

On a side note, the product is called 1,2-dibromoethane because there are two bromines (hence 'dibromo', one each on carbons 1 and 2, hence '1,2-dibromo') and that the final product has no C=C bond (hence no 'ene').

# of identical chemical groups	prefix
2	Di-
3	Tri-
4	Tetra-

GOLDEN RULE
DISPLAYED FORMULA - SHOW ALL BONDS.

✓ **LEARN**

1. Give two features of a homologous series. [2]

   Any 2 of:
   ✓ **Similar chemical properties**
   ✓ **Gradation in physical properties**
   ✓ **Same general formula**

2. Define an isomer. [2]

   ✓ **Same molecular formula**
   ✓ **Different structural formula**

3. Draw the displayed formula for propene. [1]

$$H-\overset{\displaystyle H}{\underset{\displaystyle H}{\overset{|}{\underset{|}{C}}}}-\overset{\displaystyle H}{\underset{|}{\overset{|}{C}}}=C\overset{\displaystyle H}{\underset{\displaystyle H}{\diagdown}}$$

4. Why are alkenes considered unsaturated? [1]

   ✓ **They have a double C=C bond.**

5. Describe the chemical test for alkenes. [2]

   ✓ **Add bromine water**
   ✓ **Turns from orange to colourless in the presence of alkenes**

6. Write the balanced chemical equation for the combustion of ethane. [1]

   ✓ $2CH_3CH_3 + 7O_2 \rightarrow 4CO_2 + 6H_2O$

OUR TIP

It is acceptable to write 'C_2H_6' for ethane because there is only one possible arrangement for it.

7. Name the following compounds - some of them are challenging! [8]

a)

$$H-\overset{\overset{\displaystyle H}{|}}{\underset{\underset{\displaystyle H}{|}}{C}}-\overset{\overset{\displaystyle H}{|}}{\underset{\underset{\displaystyle H}{|}}{C}}-\overset{\overset{\displaystyle H}{|}}{\underset{\underset{\displaystyle H}{|}}{C}}-H$$

b)

$$H-\overset{\overset{\displaystyle H}{|}}{\underset{\underset{\displaystyle H}{|}}{C}}-\overset{\overset{\overset{\displaystyle H}{|}}{\overset{\displaystyle C}{|}}\overset{\displaystyle H}{|}}{\underset{\underset{\displaystyle H}{|}}{C}}-\overset{\overset{\displaystyle H}{|}}{\underset{\underset{\displaystyle H}{|}}{C}}-\overset{\overset{\displaystyle H}{|}}{\underset{\underset{\displaystyle H}{|}}{C}}-H$$

c)

$$H-\overset{\overset{\displaystyle H}{|}}{\underset{\underset{\displaystyle H}{|}}{C}}-\overset{\overset{\displaystyle H}{|}}{C}=\overset{}{C}-\overset{\overset{\displaystyle H}{|}}{\underset{\underset{\displaystyle H}{|}}{C}}-H$$

d)

$$H-\overset{\overset{\displaystyle H}{|}}{\underset{\underset{\displaystyle H}{|}}{C}}-\overset{\overset{\overset{\displaystyle H}{|}}{\overset{\displaystyle C}{|}}\overset{\displaystyle H}{|}}{\underset{\underset{\overset{\displaystyle H}{|}}{\overset{\displaystyle C}{|}}\overset{\displaystyle H}{|}}{C}}-\overset{\overset{\displaystyle H}{|}}{\underset{\underset{\displaystyle H}{|}}{C}}-H$$

e)

$$H-\overset{\overset{\displaystyle H}{|}}{\underset{\underset{\displaystyle H}{|}}{C}}-\overset{\overset{\displaystyle Br}{|}}{\underset{\underset{\displaystyle Br}{|}}{C}}-\overset{\overset{\displaystyle H}{|}}{\underset{\underset{\displaystyle H}{|}}{C}}-H$$

f)

$$H-\overset{\overset{\displaystyle H}{|}}{\underset{\underset{\displaystyle Br}{|}}{C}}-\overset{\overset{\displaystyle Br}{|}}{\underset{\underset{\displaystyle H}{|}}{C}}-H$$

g)

$$\overset{H}{\underset{H}{>}}C=C\overset{H}{\underset{H}{<}}$$

h)

$$H-\overset{\overset{\displaystyle H}{|}}{\underset{\underset{\displaystyle H}{|}}{C}}-\overset{\overset{\displaystyle H}{|}}{\underset{\underset{\displaystyle H}{|}}{C}}-\overset{\overset{\displaystyle Br}{|}}{C}=C\overset{H}{\underset{H}{<}}$$

✓ **a) propane**
✓ **b) 2-methylbutane**
✓ **c) but-2-ene**
✓ **d) 2,2-dimethylpropane**
✓ **e) 2,2-dibromopropane**
✓ **f) 1,2-dibromoethane**
✓ **g) ethene**
✓ **h) 2-bromobut-1-ene**

3.2: CRUDE OIL

Here, we will be learning to:

☑ Explain how crude oil can be separated into fractions of similarly-sized hydrocarbons in a fractionating column.

☑ Recall the uses for the following fractions: refinery gases, gasoline, kerosene, diesel, fuel oil and bitumen.

☑ Describe and explain the trends in melting/boiling points and viscosity for the above fractions.

☑ Understand the reasons for catalytic cracking and recall its conditions for such.

☑ Deduce the products from the catalytic cracking of any given hydrocarbon.

☑ Explain how the combustion of hydrocarbons can lead to environmental problems.

☑ Explain how combustion of fuels contribute to the formation of nitrous oxides and sulfur dioxide, and the effects of the two gases on the environment.

☑ Describe ways to reduce the emissions of nitrous oxides and sulfur dioxide.

✓ UNDERSTAND

. . . .

CRUDE OIL

Crude oil is a mixture of hydrocarbons, and basically includes fuels you use in cars, your kitchen, ships, airplanes...etc.

Crude oil is separated in a **fractionating column** via **fractional distillation**. This splits crude oil into various **fractions** depending on their boiling points and size of molecules in each fraction. Larger hydrocarbons have higher boiling points (due to stronger intermolecular forces) and are more 'gooey' (i.e. less runny or more '**viscous**'; and slower to evaporate or less '**volatile**') for the same reasons.

This means that the smaller hydrocarbons vapourise at a lower temperature and remain in gaseous fractions higher up the fractionating column. By comparison, larger hydrocarbons remain liquid and fall down to a level in the fractionating column where temperatures are high enough for them to boil. Different hydrocarbons collect at each level, are condensed into liquids and are then tapped off.

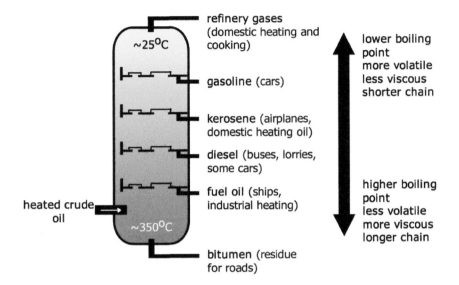

Yes, you have to learn all the names above, and the order they come in the fractionating column.

The problem with this is that the fractional distillation of crude oil produces more long-chain hydrocarbons (which are less useful) than short-chain hydrocarbons. This is where **catalytic cracking** comes in. Catalytic cracking involves using an **alumina/silica catalyst** and a high temperature of **600-700°C** to break long-chain alkanes into more useful shorter chain alkenes and alkanes by breaking the C-C covalent bonds.

Writing equations for these are easy - just make sure you've balanced the number of C and H atoms on each side. For example, we might crack $C_{18}H_{40}$ into:

$$C_{18}H_{38} \rightarrow 2C_3H_6 + 2C_4H_8 + C_4H_{10}$$

C_4H_{10} is a shorter-chain alkane; C_3H_6 and C_4H_8 are alkenes.

ENVIRONMENTAL PROBLEMS

The combustion of hydrocarbon fuels has many problems for the environment:

- **Complete combustion produces CO_2** - a greenhouse gas which can contribute to global warming.
- **Incomplete combustion produces CO** - a poisonous gas that reduces the capacity of our blood to carry oxygen around the body.
- **Nitrogen oxides (e.g. NO, NO_x)** - produced because car engines reach temperatures high enough for N_2 and O_2 to react. These contribute to **smog**, and might react with water and oxygen to form **nitric acid**, which can lead to **acid rain**. The problem is partially solved by **catalytic converters** in cars, which converts them back to N_2 gas.
- **Sulfur dioxide (SO_2)** - a by-product of hydrocarbon combustion, due to the presence of sulfur-containing compounds in fossil fuels, it can also react with water and oxygen to produce **sulfuric acid**, which also contributes to **acid rain**. This can be solved by **scrubbing** (which involves using material to absorb sulfur dioxide).

Acid rain can corrode and kill trees. It can also make the soil and lakes/rivers more acidic such that it cannot support life. Man-made structures made from limestone (calcium carbonate) and some metals might also corrode in acid rain.

✓ LEARN

1. List the crude oil fractions in increasing boiling points, and state a use for each. [12]

    ✓ **Refinery gases (e.g. domestic heating); gasoline (e.g. cars); kerosene (e.g. planes); diesel (e.g. buses); fuel oil (e.g. industrial heating); bitumen (e.g. roads).**

2. What is the process of separation that occurs in the fractionating column? [1]

    ✓ **Fractional distillation**

3. State two conditions needed for catalytic cracking. [2]

    ✓ **Alumina/silica catalyst**
    ✓ **600-700°C**

4. I cracked some decane. The products were ethene and ethane. Write a balanced chemical equation for this: [1]

    ✓ $C_{10}H_{22} \rightarrow 4C_2H_4 + C_2H_6$

5. How do nitrogen oxides and sulfur dioxide cause environmental problems and what can be done to alleviate these problems? [3]

    ✓ **Nitrogen oxides and sulfur dioxide can both react with oxygen and water to form nitric acid and sulfuric acid respectively, both of which contribute to acid rain.**
    ✓ **Catalytic converters to convert NO_x to harmless N_2 gas.**
    ✓ **Scrubbing to remove SO_2.**

3.3: SYNTHETIC POLYMERS

Here, we will be learning to:

☑ Understand the terms polymer and monomer.

☑ Understand the formation of addition polymers from alkenes, and draw the repeating units of poly(ethene), poly(propene) and poly(chloroethene).

☑ Describe uses for the above polymers and explain why they are so hard to dispose of.

☑ Understand the formation of condensation polymers such as nylon.

☑ Recall the monomers that make up nylon.

✓ UNDERSTAND

ADDITION POLYMERS

Addition polymers are formed by joining up many small, identical chemical units called **monomers**.

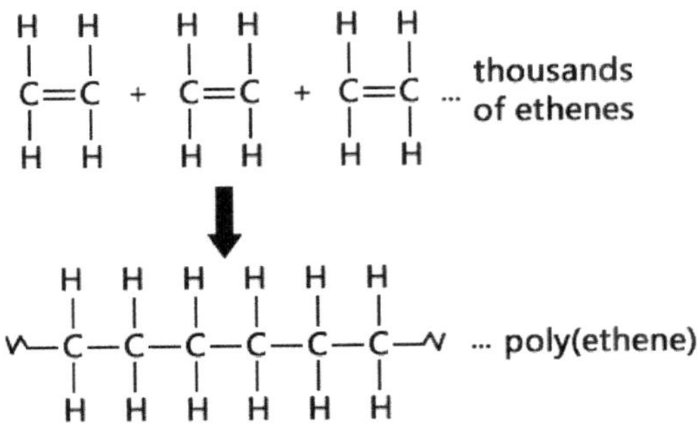

Hydrocarbons with double bonds, namely alkenes, can be polymerised. The diagram to the right illustrates this. Basically, the C=C bond breaks into a C-C bond, such that each C initially involved in the double bond can now form four covalent bonds.

The **repeating unit** basically shows the monomer of a polymer. When drawing these, you must include the 'n' and the '( )' brackets, and **horizontal lines must go through the brackets**.

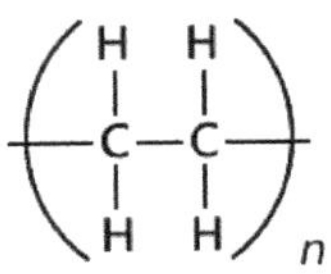

poly(ethene) 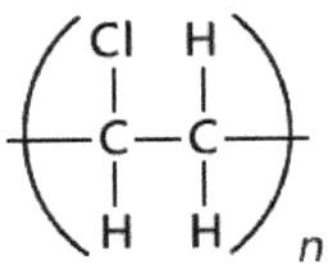   poly(chloroethene) 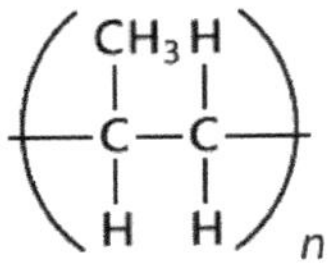   poly(propene)

Their uses:

- **Poly(ethene)** - plastic shopping bags, plastic bottles...
- **Poly(chloroethene)** - PVC for producing pipes, insulating electrical cables...
- **Poly(propene)** - fibres for carpets and clothing, making weatherproof material, ropes, plastic boxes...

Since these polymers are saturated, large and typically have unreactive functional groups (i.e. chemical groups) they are quite inert. This makes it hard to get rid of because they do not biodegrade. So **recycle** your plastics!

CONDENSATION POLYMERS

Some polymers such as **nylon** are formed by condensation polymers. This type of polymerisation produces a small molecule, such as H_2O or HCl, every time a bond is formed between two monomers.

In nylon, the monomers are **1,6-diaminohexane** and **hexanedioic acid**.

✓ LEARN

1. Draw the displayed formula of:

a) Poly(ethene) [1]

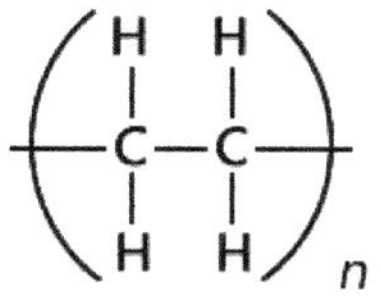

b) Poly(propene) [1]

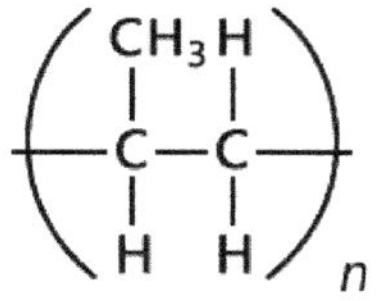

c) Poly(chloroethene)* [1]

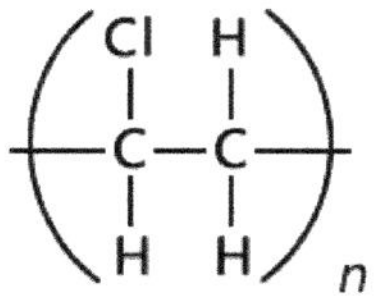

2. State some uses for the following polymers:

    a) Poly(ethene) [1]

        ✓ **Plastic shopping bags, plastic bottles...etc.**

    b) Poly(propene) [1]

        ✓ **Ropes, crates, carpet/clothing fibres, weatherproof materials...etc.**

    c) Poly(chloroethene)* [1]

        ✓ **Plastic pipes, electrical insulation...etc.**

3. Why are addition polymers hard to dispose of? [2]

    ✓ **Addition polymers are hard to dispose of because they do not easily biodegrade.**
    ✓ **This is because the polyalkenes do not contain functional groups that may react - they are large, inert and saturated.**

4. Name the two monomers of nylon.* [2]

    ✓ **1,6-diaminohexane**
    ✓ **Hexanedioic acid**

OUR TIP

What if they asked you to draw the nylon monomers? If you remember the names, then drawing it should be easier - clue's in the name, although these ideas **do go beyond IGCSE**. You can guess that **hex**ane means an alkane with 6 carbons, all C-C single bonds. An amine is an NH_2, so '1,6-diamino' means 2 amines, 1 each on carbon 1 and carbon 6. 'Oic' means a carbon at the end has C-OH and C=O bonds. '**Di**oic' means there are two of such carbons. 'Hexane' means a total of 6 carbons. So 'hexandioic' means 6 carbons, with the ones on opposite ends forming C-OH and C=O bonds instead of C-H bonds.

✓ SECTION 3: MANIPULATE

(Total: 37 marks)

These questions will require you to utilise what you know from multiple chapters of this section. Try your best!

1. Tim works at the gas station in London, to fund his PhD in Organic Chemistry all the way at Winterfell College, University of Westeros.

    a) Name a fraction of crude oil Tim might find in the gas station. [1]
    b) The oil in his gas station consists only of alkanes. Why might alkanes be considered saturated? [1]
    c) Alkanes are a homologous series. State two features of a homologous series. [2]
    d) Tim doesn't know that he only works with alkanes. He thinks he works with alkenes. How can he confirm that he only works with alkanes? [2]
    e) There will always be incomplete combustion in the car engines, which produces a gaseous product. What is this gaseous product and why might it be detrimental to Tim's health? [2]
    f) The heat in car engines also produces nitrogen oxides. Give two ways in which this might affect the climate, and name one way in which nitrogen oxide emissions can be removed from cars. [2]

2. John is sitting his first year Chemistry exams at Barden University. He turns to the 'Organic Chemistry' section...

    a) Fill this diagram with the correct fractions: [6]

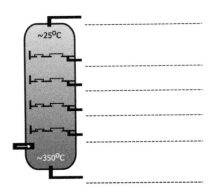

b) What process of separation is shown in the diagram? [1]

c) The process shown above produces lots of longer chained hydrocarbons of little use. How can John produce more useful shorter hydrocarbons, and name two conditions needed for the process? [3]

d) His method ends up producing three alkenes: **i)** but-2-ene, **ii)** ethene and **iii)** pent-1-ene. Draw the displayed formula for each of them. [3]

e) Draw two isomers of C_4H_{10}. [2]

3. Mike is the manager of the fast-food chain *Los Pollos Hermanos*, Springfield branch. His restaurant is running out of supplies.

a) He needs to order some uniform for the new interns. These are made of nylon. Name the two monomers that make up nylon.* [2]

b) What type of polymerisation does nylon undergo, and which other molecule is produced?* [2]

c) Mike also orders more plastic bags for takeaways. Name the polymer that these plastic bags might be made of and draw the repeating unit. [2]

d) Name the following: [4]

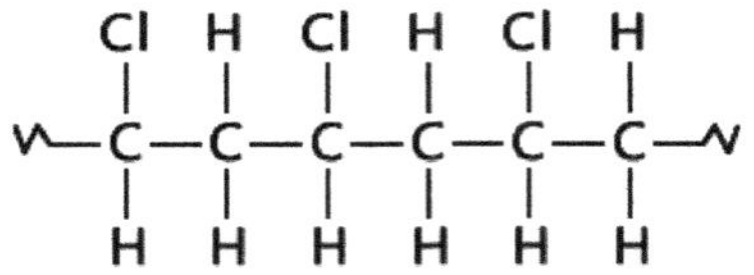

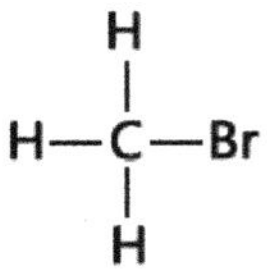

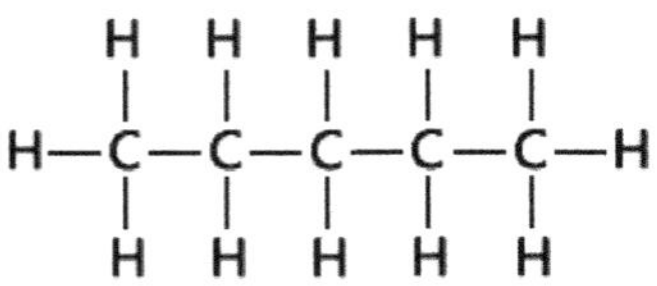

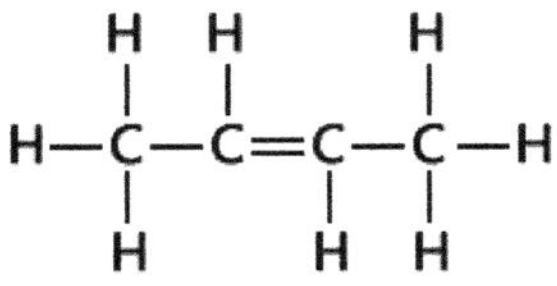

e) Mike disposes of his plastic bags into the ocean to annoy his rival, Mr. Krabs of Bikini Bottom. He knows that these plastic bags will not easily biodegrade. Explain why not. [1]

f) Name the type of reaction that occurs between methane and bromine in the presence of UV light. [1]

SECTION 4:

PHYSICAL & INDUSTRIAL CHEMISTRY

4.1: RATES OF REACTION

Here, we will be learning to:

- ☑ Investigate and explain the effects of surface area, concentration, temperature and the presence of a catalyst on the rate of reaction.
- ☑ Define activation energy.
- ☑ Explain how catalysts increase rate of reaction and illustrate this using a reaction profile.

✓ UNDERSTAND

The **rate of reaction** is defined as the change in concentration of a reactant or product per unit time. We can investigate the factors that affect the rate of reaction using experiments such as the one described below.

Place an empty beaker on a balance and 'zero' it. Add a fixed amount of HCl(aq) and add an excess of calcium carbonate marble chips. We know that CO_2 will be produced, so we can measure the **rate of reaction** by measuring the mass of CO_2 produced per second (via loss of mass in beaker). We can use this setup to investigate factors that affect the rate of reaction:

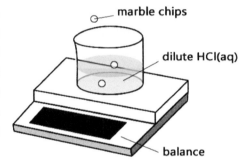

marble chips

dilute HCl(aq)

balance

- **Surface area:** the larger the surface area, the higher the **frequency of successful collisions** between the two reagents. We can investigate surface area by comparing rates using the same mass of powdered $CaCO_3$, the original marble chips and big lumps of $CaCO_3$ for example.
- **Concentration:** If we increase the concentration, we're increasing the number of reagent molecules available in a given volume, so more product is formed. There will also be more successful collisions per second, hence rate increases. We can alter the HCl(aq) concentration to investigate this.
- **Pressure of gases:** the higher the pressure, the closer together the reagents will be. Again, a higher rate of reaction is achieved due to the higher frequency of

successful collisions. (Obviously, this experiment does not involve gases so we cannot investigate pressure).

- **Temperature:** high temperatures increase the kinetic energy of particles (i.e. they move faster), increasing the frequency of collisions. More importantly, a greater proportion of molecules possess the activation energy [activation energy in bold], so a greater proportion of these collisions are successful.
- **Using a catalyst:** a catalyst increases the rate of reaction by providing an **alternative route** of **lower activation energy**, without being chemically changed or 'used up' at the end of the reaction. We will get to what this means shortly.

GOLDEN RULE

CATALYSTS DO NOT DIRECTLY LOWER THE ACTIVATION ENERGY REQUIRED FOR A GIVEN REACTION TO TAKE PLACE. THEY INSTEAD PROVIDE AN ALTERNATIVE ROUTE FOR THE REACTION THAT REQUIRES A LOWER ACTIVATION ENERGY.

This rule may seem very picky and slightly confusing, but it is important that you understand that a catalyst effectively acts like a short-cut for the reaction. Before the catalyst is added, that short cut is blocked and so the reaction has to take the long route. However, the catalyst is able to remove that road-block, enabling the reaction to take the short-cut. As such, the catalyst provides an alternative route for the reaction that requires less energy.

Our results should show something like this:

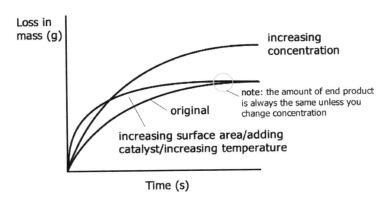

Note: The curve for 'increasing concentration' is higher than the 'original' curve because we've used an excess of $CaCO_3$. If we hadn't used an excess, then our curve might look different because the $CaCO_3$ will be used up over time.

WHAT ARE 'SUCCESSFUL' COLLISIONS?

A successful collision is one in which the two reactants collide with enough energy to overcome the activation energy. The **activation energy** is the minimum energy required for a reaction to occur when two particles collide.

To reiterate, catalysts provide an alternative route of lower activation energy - in other words, they provide a different pathway from the reactants to the products, one which requires less energy. This is shown in the energy profile to the right.

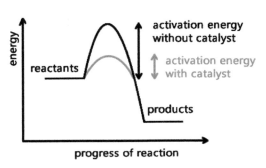

✓ LEARN

1. The diagram shows the change in concentration of a product over time, and can be used as a measure of the rate of reaction:

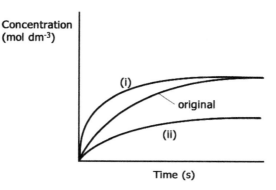

a) Which two factors might have been investigated to produce curves (i) and (ii)? [2]

   ✓ **For (i) any 1 of: adding catalyst; increasing surface area; or increasing temperature.**

   ✓ **For (ii) decreasing concentration of reagent.**

b) What does a catalyst do and how does it work? [2]

   ✓ **It increases the rate of reaction without being chemically changed or used up.**

   ✓ **It provides an alternative route for a reaction that requires a lower activation energy.**

c) How does temperature affect the rate of reaction? [2]

   ✓ **It affects the kinetic energy of the reactant particles**

   ✓ **...which can then affect the frequency of collisions with energy ≥ the activation energy.**

4.2: EQUILIBRIA

Here, we will be learning to:

☑ Know that some reactions are reversible, and be familiar with examples such as the hydration of anhydrous copper(II) sulfate crystals and the reaction between ammonia and hydrogen chloride to form ammonium chloride.

☑ Use Le Chatelier's Principle to predict the position of equilibrium in a reversible reaction under changing conditions.

✓ UNDERSTAND

It's possible for many reactions to proceed both backwards and forwards, thus, be **reversible**. This is denoted by the '$\rightleftharpoons$' instead of the '$\rightarrow$' arrow.

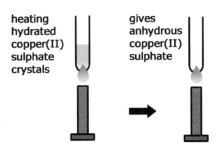

heating hydrated copper(II) sulphate crystals

gives anhydrous copper(II) sulphate

For example, when you add water to the copper sulfate, it turns blue as water molecules get 'locked' up inside their crystals. When you heat it, these water molecules get removed, and so the copper(II) sulfate turns white again.

hydrated copper(II) sulfate $\rightleftharpoons$ anhydrous copper(II) sulfate + water

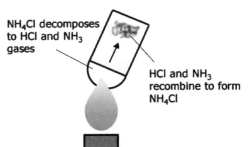

NH$_4$Cl decomposes to HCl and NH$_3$ gases

HCl and NH$_3$ recombine to form NH$_4$Cl

The reaction between ammonia and hydrogen chloride to form ammonium chloride is also reversible:

$$NH_3(g) + HCl(g) \rightleftharpoons NH_4Cl(s)$$

This is also a **neutralisation reaction**.

LE CHATELIER'S PRINCIPLE

When a reversible reaction is occurring in a **closed system** (that is, reactants and products cannot escape), it will reach a **dynamic equilibrium**. This is when both the **forward and backward reactions are occurring at equal rates**.

Think of walking down an ascending escalator at the same speed the escalator is moving up, or perhaps running on a treadmill. In both cases, the 'forward' and 'backward' events are occurring, but you are not moving overall.

However, **Le Chatelier's principle** states that there are changes you can make to a closed reversible reaction, to shift the position of the equilibrium such that it might produce more product or reactant:

> **If a change is made to the conditions of a system in equilibrium, the position of the equilibrium will shift to oppose the change.**

The position of equilibrium basically refers to the relative amounts of reactants and products. The concept will be better understood if we consider an example:

$$2A + B \rightleftharpoons C + D \qquad \Delta H = -X \text{ kJ mol}^{-1}$$

The position of equilibrium will change if we tamper with the conditions!

- **Adding more B** - will cause the system to oppose the change by decreasing B. This is done by shifting the position of equilibrium to the right, producing more C and D.
- **Removing B** - will cause the system to oppose the change by increasing B. Thus, the equilibrium will shift to the left (by favouring the backward reaction), and produce more A and B.
- **Increasing the temperature** – briefly, ΔH denotes **enthalpy change**, a term used to describe the energy change of a reaction under constant pressure (more in Section 5.3). If ΔH is negative, it means the forward reaction is exothermic. It also means the backward reaction is endothermic. If we increase the temperature, the system will oppose the change by decreasing the temperature.

This is done by shifting the position of equilibrium backwards, in the endothermic direction, producing more A and B.

- **Decreasing the temperature** - will cause the system to oppose the change by increasing the temperature. This is done by favouring the forward, exothermic reaction, thus producing more C and D.

- **Increasing pressure** - the system will oppose the change by decreasing the pressure. In such a closed system, this can only be done by favouring the reaction that produces the least number of molecules. We know the forward reaction produces 2 moles of molecules (we will get to this in the next section, but just treat it as a ratio) whereas the backward reaction produces 3 moles. Thus, when you decrease the pressure, the forward reaction is favoured, so the equilibrium shifts right, producing more C and D.

- **Decreasing pressure** - the system will oppose the change by increasing pressure. This is done by increasing the number of molecules. Hence the equilibrium will shift left, producing more A and B.

- **Adding a catalyst** - this increases the rates of the forward and backward reactions by the same amount, so the position of equilibrium does not change.

✓ LEARN

1. Consider the reaction: $NH_3(g) + HCl(g) \rightleftharpoons NH_4Cl(s)$ $\Delta H = $ -176 kJ mol^{-1}
   What happens to the position of equilibrium if...

   a) The temperature is decreased? [2]

   > ✓ **The equilibrium will shift to increase the temperature.**
   > ✓ **Since the forward reaction is exothermic, the equilibrium will shift right.**

   b) We remove the NH$_4$Cl as it is being formed? [1]

   > ✓ **The equilibrium will shift right to oppose the change by increasing the concentration of NH$_4$Cl.**

2. Consider the reaction: $3H_2(g) + N_2(g) \rightleftharpoons 2NH_3(g)$ $\Delta H = $ -92 kJ mol^{-1}
   What happens to the yield (amount) of NH$_3$ produced if...

   a) The temperature is increased? [3]

   > ✓ **The equilibrium will shift to decrease the temperature.**
   > ✓ **Since the forward reaction is exothermic, the equilibrium will shift left.**
   > ✓ **Hence the yield of NH$_3$ will decrease.**

   b) The pressure is decreased? [3]

   > ✓ **The equilibrium will shift to increase the pressure.**
   > ✓ **Since there are more moles of gas on the left than the right (4 moles on the left as opposed to 2 on the right), the equilibrium will shift left.**
   > ✓ **This decreases the yield of NH$_3$.**

   c) Adding a catalyst? [2]

   > ✓ **No change**
   > ✓ **Rates of forward and backward reactions increase by the same amount.**

4.3: ELECTROLYSIS

Here, we will be learning to:

☑ Explain why ionic compounds conduct electricity only when molten or in solution, and why covalent compounds do not.

☑ Test for whether a given substance might be an electrolyte.

☑ Investigate the electrolysis of molten salts (e.g. lead(II) bromide) and aqueous solutions (e.g. copper(II) sulfate and dilute sulfuric acid).

☑ Write ionic half equations for electrolysis experiments.

✓ UNDERSTAND

Electrolysis is a redox reaction produced by passing an electric current through an ionic compound that is either molten or in solution. It leads to the formation of new substances. An **electrolyte** is a substance that undergoes electrolysis.

An **electric current** is simply a flow of electrons or ions. Such a concept is important because we can infer that **covalent compounds are not electrolytes** (they have no free moving electrons, nor do they contain ions). On the other hand, **ionic compounds can conduct electricity only when molten or in a solution** because then the ions separate and become mobile.

We can distinguish between electrolytes and non-electrolytes:

1. Dissolve or melt substance.
2. Put a **conductivity tester** in the substance. This is essentially a simple circuit.
3. If bulb lights up, it means the substance 'completes' the circuit, indicating the presence of mobile, charged particles, showing that the substance is an electrolyte.

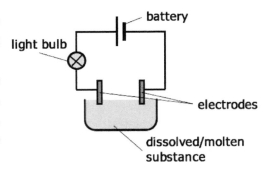

An electrolysis setup consists of:

- **Carbon electrodes** because these are fairly un-reactive.
- The positive electrode is called the **anode**. It lacks electrons because they've moved to the cathode (hence there is a net positive charge).
- The negative electrode is called the **cathode**. It has an abundance of electrons (hence the negative charge).

ELECTROLYSIS OF MOLTEN SALTS

A simple example of electrolysis involves **molten lead(II) bromide**:

> **OUR TIP**
> **Remember:** "I used to have a girlfriend called Cath. She was a very negative influence."

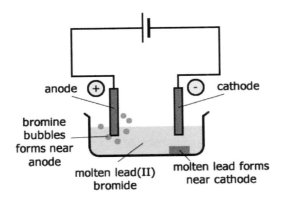

anode (+)   cathode

bromine bubbles forms near anode

molten lead(II) bromide

molten lead forms near cathode

- When molten, the lead (Pb^{2+}) ions and bromide (Br^-) ions are able to move.
- The **Pb^{2+} ions** become attracted to the cathode and get reduced. These ions gain 2 electrons, hence becoming lead atoms.
- The **Br^- ions** become attracted to the anode and gets oxidised. These ions lose 1 electron, becoming Br. Then, 2Br join together to form Br_2, as bromine is diatomic. This bromine escapes as a gas.

The ionic half-equations:

At the anode: **$2Br^-(aq) \rightarrow Br_2(g) + 2e^-$** (oxidation)
At the cathode: **$Pb^{2+}(aq) + 2e^- \rightarrow Pb(s)$** (reduction)

ELECTROLYSIS OF AQUEOUS SOLUTIONS

When you electrolyse **aqueous solutions**, things are different because you have to consider the water molecules too. Water is strange in that it can also ionise to form hydrogen and hydroxide ions, thus making it a weak electrolyte:

$$H_2O \rightleftharpoons H^+ + OH^-$$

As a result, we will have additional ions in the solution to be electrolysed. The ions that more easily oxidise or reduce will be the ones that do so at the anode and cathode respectively. How do we know which ones these are? In general:

- If the metal is more reactive than hydrogen, it gains electrons less readily (because it loses them more easily). Hence, hydrogen ions from water will be reduced instead. These pair up to form H_2 gas.
- If the metal is below hydrogen, you get the metal produced.
- If you have solutions of halides, you get the halogen produced because these oxidise more readily than OH^- ions.
- With other negative ions such as sulfates, oxygen will be produced because OH^- ions oxidise instead.

potassium
sodium
lithium
calcium
magnesium
aluminium
carbon
zinc
iron
hydrogen
copper
silver
gold

Admittedly, this section is tough, so make sure you reread this until you understand it. If not, ask your teacher!

Let's look at the electrolysis of **copper(II) sulfate solution**:

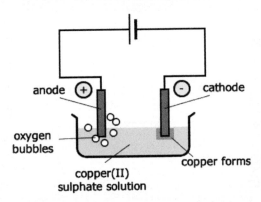

- Copper is less reactive than hydrogen so the Cu^{2+} ions get reduced. A coat of copper metal forms at the cathode: $Cu^{2+}(aq) + 2e^- \rightarrow Cu(s)$
- O_2 gas is discharged because the SO_4^{2-} ions are harder to oxidise, so OH^- ions get oxidised instead: $4OH^-(aq) \rightarrow 2H_2O(l) + 4e^- + O_2(g)$

Something interesting happens when you leave the setup for longer. The H^+ and SO_4^{2-} ions aren't being discharged and so what happens is, the solution becomes **sulfuric acid**. And that starts electrolysing...

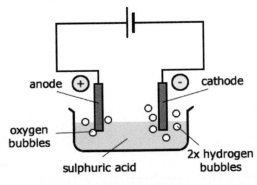

- As the H^+ would be the only anions left, they get reduced and discharged: $2H^+(aq) + 2e^- \rightarrow H_2(g)$
- O_2 gas is still discharged because the SO_4^{2-} ions are harder to oxidise. Remember the whole thing is in solution, so there is still water (which dissociates to OH^- and H^+ ions) so OH^- ions get oxidised instead: $4OH^-(aq) \rightarrow 2H_2O(l) + 4e^- + O_2(g)$

Now, if we balance both equations (by equating the number of electrons):

$$4H^+(aq) + 4e^- \rightarrow 2H_2(g)$$
$$4OH^-(aq) \rightarrow 2H_2O(l) + 4e^- + O_2(g)$$

We can see that for every four e^- that flows around the circuit, one oxygen molecule and two hydrogen molecules are produced. In other words, **twice as many hydrogen molecules are produced** compared to the oxygen molecules.

Note: This whole second part about the electrolysis of sulfuric acid could be tested independently of the first part about copper(II) sulfate, so don't be shocked if you are simply asked about the electrolysis of H_2SO_4 as all of this still applies.

Great! At this stage we have been equipped with lots of knowledge about rates of reactions, equilibrium and electrolysis. All these come together in the next section about industrial processes, where such knowledge enables us to maximise the yield of our products...

OUR TIP

Metals ending with **'ium'** and zinc produce H_2; those without the 'ium' are produced themselves. Non-metals ending with **'ate'** or **'oxide'** produce O_2; those with **'ide'** produce themselves.

✓ LEARN

1. Define:

   a) Electrolysis [1]

   > ✓ **Electrolysis is a redox reaction produced by passing an electric current through an ionic compound that is either molten or in solution.**

   b) An electric current [1]

   > ✓ **Flow of ions or electrons**

2. I have two beakers. One contains potassium nitrate solution and the other is a glucose solution ($C_6H_{12}O_6$). I place a conductivity tester in each beaker. What would I expect to see and why? [3]

   > ✓ **Light bulb lights up with the potassium nitrate solution but not the glucose solution.**
   > ✓ **Potassium nitrate is an ionic compound, thus in solution, it contains mobile K^+ and NO_3^- ions that can flow around the circuit and complete it.**
   > ✓ **Glucose does not dissociate into mobile ions because the molecules are bonded covalently.**

3. I electrolyse some molten zinc chloride ($ZnCl_2$).

a) What do I observe at the anode and cathode? [2]

✓ **Zinc metal will sink to the bottom below the cathode.**
✓ **Gas bubbles will be produced at the anode.**

b) What gas is produced at the anode, and how would you test to verify your answer? [2]

✓ **Chlorine**
✓ **Turns damp blue litmus paper red, and then bleaches it white.**

c) Write the ionic half equations for each electrode (specify electrode) and state the processes occurring at each: [4]

✓ **Cathode: $Zn^{2+} + 2e^- \rightarrow Zn$; reduction**
✓ **Anode: $2Cl^- \rightarrow Cl_2 + 2e^-$; oxidation**

4. I electrolyse some aqueous silver(I) nitrate.*

a) What do I observe at the anode and cathode? [2]

✓ **Silver will form and cover the cathode because it is lower than hydrogen on the reactivity series, hence it is more easily reduced.**
✓ **Gas bubbles will be produced at the anode.**

b) Write the ionic half equations for each electrode (specify electrode). [2]

✓ **Cathode: $Ag^+ + e^- \rightarrow Ag$**
✓ **Anode: $4OH^- \rightarrow 2H_2O + 4e^- + O_2$**

5. I electrolyse some sulfuric acid - a diagram of this is shown below:*

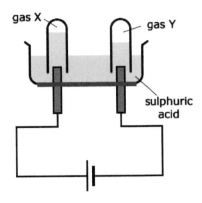

a) Label gases X and Y [2]

   ✓ **X - oxygen; Y – hydrogen**

b) Write the ionic half equations for each electrode (specify electrode). [2]

   ✓ **Cathode:** $2H^+ + 2e^- \rightarrow H_2$
   ✓ **Anode:** $4OH^- \rightarrow 2H_2O + 4e^- + O_2$

c) Why is twice as much Y produced as X? [1]

   ✓ **For every four e⁻ that flows around the circuit, one oxygen molecule and two hydrogen molecules are produced.**

4.4: INDUSTRIAL PROCESSES

Here, we will be learning to:

☑   Understand the electrolysis of brine to manufacture chlorine and sodium hydroxide.

☑   Describe uses for chlorine and sodium hydroxide.

☑   Understand the use of electrolysis to extract aluminium and the problems encountered by such in the industry.

☑   Describe uses for aluminium and relate those to the properties of aluminium.

☑   Understand the manufacture of ammonia via the Haber Process, and explain the choice of temperature, pressure and the usage of a catalyst.

☑   Describe uses for ammonia.

☑   Understand the manufacture of sulfuric acid via the Contact Process and describe uses for sulfuric acid.

☑   Understand how iron is extracted in the blast furnace, and how silicon dioxide impurities are removed using limestone.

☑   Describe uses for iron.

☑   Understand that the differences in methods for extracting aluminium and iron are related to their positions in the reactivity series.

☑   Explain how ethanol can be manufactured via the hydration of ethene or fermentation, and suggest the advantages and disadvantages of both methods.

✓ UNDERSTAND

· ·

Right! This chapter brings in everything we've learnt so far and explains how it's all utilised in industry. Admittedly, learning all of the facts and figures about each process is a little dull. However, if you've understood everything so far, you should find that these industrial processes come as a logical progression from the theory you've been learning. With our minds fresh from our newfound understanding of electrolysis, let's start with that!

ELECTROLYSIS OF BRINE TO MAKE CHLORINE AND SODIUM HYDROXIDE

The electrolysis of brine (concentrated sodium chloride solution) takes place in a diaphragm cell - which is basically an electrolysis setup with a few added modifications.

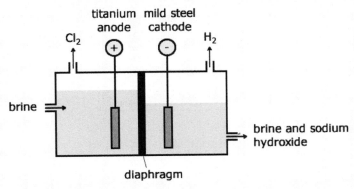

- Chlorine gets oxidised at the anode: $2Cl^-(aq) \rightarrow Cl_2(g) + 2e^-$
- Hydrogen gets reduced at the cathode: $2H^+(aq) + 2e^- \rightarrow H_2(g)$

Hence, what remains in the solution are OH⁻ ions and Na⁺ ions - in other words, a sodium hydroxide solution. The chlorine gas is collected. Both have their uses:

- **Sodium hydroxide** is used for making bleach, paper and soap.
- **Chlorine** is used also in the manufacture of bleach, hydrochloric acid and for sterilising water supplies such as in swimming pools.

The chlorine gas and hydrogen gas are kept separate by a **semi-permeable diaphragm** to prevent them reacting with one another to form hydrogen chloride (which can be explosive). Also, the level of brine on the left is always higher than the right, to prevent sodium hydroxide mixing with the chlorine, which can form bleach.

EXTRACTION OF ALUMINIUM

Many of the processes of metal extraction at IGCSE rely on an understanding of the reactivity series. Aluminium is found in **bauxite ore** in the form of aluminium oxide. It is extracted via the electrolysis of **purified aluminium oxide** dissolved in a **molten**

cryolite solvent. The molten cryolite **reduces the operating temperature** (because aluminium oxide itself has a very high melting point, but the mixture has a lower melting point).

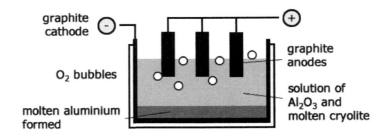

- Oxygen gets oxidised at the anode: $2O^{2-} \rightarrow O_2 + 4e^-$
- Aluminium gets reduced at the cathode: $Al^{3+} + 3e^- \rightarrow Al$

Some practical issues:

- ✗ The **graphite anodes need to be replaced** regularly because they react with the oxygen produced to form carbon dioxide.
- ✗ The **cost of electricity** is a major factor because it requires a high current (in the hundred thousands of Amps).

Common uses of aluminium include:

- **Making saucepans** - because it conducts heat, is resistant to corrosion and has a low density.
- **Making airplanes** - because it has a low density, is strong and is resistant to corrosion.
- **Making soft drink cans and other packaging materials** - same reasons as above, plus it is malleable so it can be easily shaped.

THE HABER PROCESS

The **Haber process** is used to make ammonia. **Nitrogen** is obtained from the air and **hydrogen** is obtained either from natural gas or cracking hydrocarbons. The process involves a

CONDITIONS:
- ☑ **450°C**
- ☑ **200 atm**
- ☑ **Iron catalyst**

chemical equilibrium:

$$N_2(g) + 3H_2(g) \rightleftharpoons 2NH_3(g) \qquad \Delta H = -92 \text{ kJ mol}^{-1}$$

The ammonia is **cooled and condensed into a liquid** (while the N_2 and H_2 remain as gases) before being tapped off. This means any unused N_2 and H_2 can be **recycled** (when you remove the NH_3, the equilibrium will oppose the change by producing more!). Some pointers:

- Lowering the temperature would increase the yield of ammonia because the forward reaction is exothermic. However, if the temperature was too low, then the rate of reaction would be very slow. Hence, 450°C is a **compromise** between high rate and high yield. The cost of heating is also a factor.
- Pressure is also a compromise. Ideally, we would increase the pressure to produce more ammonia (because the equilibrium would shift right to produce less moles of gas). However, the high costs of this, due to the energy required to pressurise further, means this is not profitable.
- The iron catalyst has no effect on the position of the equilibrium and is simply there to increase the rates of the forward and backward reactions.

Uses of ammonia include manufacturing **fertilisers** (in the form of ammonium nitrate) and **nitric acid**. Ammonium nitrate is formed from the reaction between ammonia and nitric acid.

$$NH_3 + HNO_3 \rightarrow NH_4NO_3$$

THE CONTACT PROCESS

The **Contact process** is used to make sulfuric acid for manufacturing **detergents**, **fertilisers** and **paint**.

Sulfur dioxide is formed from burning sulfur in air:

$$S(s) + O_2(g) \rightarrow SO_2(g)$$

CONDITIONS:
- ☑ **450°C**
- ☑ **2 atm**
- ☑ **Vanadium(V) oxide catalyst**

An excess of air is burned with the sulfur dioxide to make sulfur trioxide:

$$2SO_2(g) + O_2(g) \rightleftharpoons 2SO_3(g) \qquad \Delta H = -196 \text{ kJ mol}^{-1}$$

- The temperature again, is a compromise between yield and rate of reaction.
- A higher pressure favours the forward reaction, but a high enough yield is produced at 2 atm anyway.
- Again, a catalyst is used to increase the rate of reaction.

Reacting sulfur trioxide with water is not a good idea because it will produce an uncontrollable fog of concentrated sulfuric acid. Instead, it is dissolved in concentrated sulfuric acid to form **oleum** (or fuming sulfuric acid):

$$SO_3(g) + H_2SO_4(aq) \rightarrow H_2S_2O_7(l)$$

Oleum is then reacted with water to produce sulfuric acid:

$$H_2S_2O_7(l) + H_2O(l) \rightarrow 2H_2SO_4(aq)$$

THE BLAST FURNACE

Iron is extracted from **haematite** which is impure iron(III) oxide. Coke (i.e. carbon) and limestone are also thrown in the furnace.

Coke burns in O_2 to form CO_2. This reaction is strongly exothermic. At high temperatures, the carbon dioxide is reduced by more carbon to give carbon monoxide.

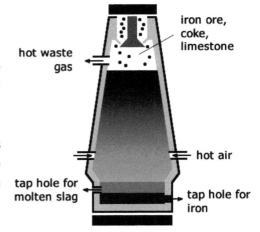

$$C(s) + O_2(g) \rightarrow CO_2(g)$$
$$C(s) + CO_2(g) \rightarrow 2CO(g)$$

CO is the **main reducing agent**, although carbon can also reduce the iron(III) oxide because the carbon (in both CO and C) can displace the iron:

$$Fe_2O_3(s) + 3CO(g) \rightarrow 2Fe(l) + 3CO_2(g)$$
$$2Fe_2O_3(s) + 3C(s) \rightarrow 4Fe(l) + 3CO_2(g)$$

The heat of the furnace causes the limestone to thermally decompose to form CaO and CO_2. The CaO reacts with silicon dioxide (one of the impurities found in haematite) to form **calcium silicate**, which melts and forms **molten slag**:

$$CaCO_3(s) \rightarrow CaO(s) + CO_2(g)$$
$$SiO_2(s) + CaO(s) \rightarrow CaSiO_3(s)$$

Iron from the blast furnace is quite brittle because of carbon impurities. As such, it is usually converted into steel, with a lower carbon content, by blowing oxygen into the iron. This oxygen reacts with the carbon to form carbon monoxide and carbon dioxide. Enough oxygen is used to obtain steel with the desired carbon content. Other metals, such as chromium and nickel, are often added to produce **alloys** with specific, desired properties.

Type of Steel	Iron Alloyed With	Properties	Uses
Low Carbon Steel	Roughly 0.25% carbon	Malleable	Car bodies
High Carbon Steel	Up to 2.5% carbon	Hard	Cutting tools
Stainless Steel	Chromium and nickel	Resistant to corrosion	Cutlery, sinks

MANUFACTURING ETHANOL

There are two main ways in which ethanol is produced:

CONDITIONS:
☑ **300°C**
☑ **60-70 atm**
☑ **Phosphoric acid catalyst**

- Hydration of ethene (i.e. reacting with steam).
- Fermentation of glucose.

The first method is a **hydration**:

$$C_2H_4(g) + H_2O(g) \rightleftharpoons C_2H_5OH(g) \qquad \Delta H = \text{-45 kJ mol}^{-1}$$

The ethanol formed is cooled and condensed, and the rest of the unused ethene is recycled back.

- Again the 'high' temperature is a compromise - to increase the rate of reaction despite reducing yield slightly.
- Again, the 'high' pressure is also a compromise - an increase would shift the equilibrium right, but it will also become more expensive. Furthermore, high pressure can cause the ethene to **polymerise**.

CONDITIONS:
☑ **30°C**
☑ **No oxygen**
☑ **Yeast catalyst**
☑ **Aqueous solution**

The second method is **fermentation**. Yeast is left in the absence of oxygen, with a sugar solution such as glucose. It will **respire anaerobically** (i.e. respire without oxygen):

$$C_6H_{12}O_6(aq) \rightarrow 2C_2H_5OH(aq) + 2CO_2(g)$$

Eventually the build-up of ethanol denatures the enzymes in yeast cells. The ethanol formed is **impure**, but it can be purified via fractional distillation.

The specific manufacturing method depends on factors such as the **availability of crude oil** (the raw material from which ethene is produced) or **sugar cane**, and **operating costs**. Both have their advantages and disadvantages.

Hydration	Fermentation
✓ Very **quick** process. ✓ **Continuous process** - more efficient. ✓ Produces **purer** ethanol ✗ **Higher operating costs** (e.g. energy costs, maintenance costs...etc.). ✗ Uses **non-renewable** resources such as crude oil.	✗ **Slower** process (several days). ✗ **Batch process** - completed reaction mixture has to be removed, and a new one set up. ✗ Ethanol produced is **impure**. ✓ **Cheaper** (e.g. because of lower temperatures). ✓ Uses **renewable resources** - sugar cane can be re-grown easily.

Finally, ethanol can be dehydrated using **heated aluminium oxide** as a catalyst:

CONDITIONS:
☑ **Aluminium oxide catalyst**

$$C_2H_5OH(g) \rightarrow C_2H_4(g) + H_2O(g)$$

Phew! We've finally made it through that section!

✓ LEARN

1. Sodium hydroxide and chlorine are produced industrially via the electrolysis of brine, using a diaphragm cell:*

   a) Name a use each for sodium hydroxide and chlorine. [2]

   - ✓ **For sodium hydroxide, any 1 of: manufacturing bleach, paper, soap.**
   - ✓ **For chlorine, any 1 of: manufacturing bleach, sterilising water supplies, manufacturing hydrochloric acid.**

   b) Write the ionic half equations for each electrode (specify electrode). [2]

   - ✓ **Cathode: $2H^+ + 2e^- \rightarrow H_2$**
   - ✓ **Anode: $2Cl^- \rightarrow Cl_2 + 2e^-$**

   c) Why must hydrogen and chlorine be separated? [1]

   - ✓ **To prevent both from reacting to form hydrogen chloride (which can be explosive).**

2. Aluminium is also extracted using electrolysis:

   a) Explain the role of the molten cryolite. [1]

   - ✓ **Serves as a solvent for purified Al_2O_3 to decrease operating temperatures, because the melting point of Al_2O_3 is very high.**

   b) Why do the carbon electrodes need replacing? [1]

   - ✓ **It reacts with the O_2 produced to give CO_2 gas.**

c) Write the ionic half equations for each electrode (specify electrode). [2]

   ✓ **Cathode:** $Al^{3+} + 3e^- \rightarrow Al$
   ✓ **Anode:** $2O^{2-} \rightarrow O_2 + 4e^-$

3. The iron blast furnace is used to extract iron from haematite:

   a) Explain the role of coke and include two equations to show it. [3]

   ✓ $C(s) + O_2(g) \rightarrow CO_2(g)$
   ✓ $C(s) + CO_2(g) \rightarrow 2CO(g)$
   ✓ **CO is the main reducing agent, which reduces Fe_2O_3 into Fe.**

   b) Write the chemical equation for the formation of iron from its oxide in the blast furnace: [1]

   ✓ $3CO + Fe_2O_3 \rightarrow 2Fe + 3CO_2$

   c) One of the impurities is silicon dioxide. Explain how this is removed. [2]

   ✓ **It reacts with CaO to form calcium silicate, which melts to the bottom of the blast furnace as molten slag. This is tapped off.**
   ✓ **CaO is formed from the thermal decomposition of limestone, which is added to the blast furnace.**

4. Fertilisers and nitric acid are made from ammonia.

   a) State three conditions used in the Haber process. [3]

   ✓ **450°C.**
   ✓ **200 atm.**
   ✓ **Iron catalyst.**

   b) Why is it not profitable or practical to have a lower temperature? [1]

   ✓ **Rate of reaction would be too slow**

c) How does iron affect the position of equilibrium? [1]

   ✓ **It doesn't**

5. There are two methods of ethanol production used in the industry.*

a) State three conditions needed for the hydration of ethene. [3]

   ✓ **300°C.**
   ✓ **60-70 atm.**
   ✓ **Phosphoric acid catalyst.**

b) Write the chemical equation for the hydration of ethene: [1]

   ✓ $C_2H_4 + H_2O \rightarrow C_2H_5OH$

c) Write the chemical equation for the fermentation of glucose. [1]

   ✓ $C_6H_{12}O_6 \rightarrow 2C_2H_5OH + 2CO_2$

d) State one factor that might determine which method of ethanol production is used in a country. [1]

   ✓ **E.g. availability of sugar cane/oil.**

e) State one advantage and one disadvantage of the hydration of ethene over fermentation. [2]

   ✓ **Any 1 of: purer ethanol; continuous process so more efficient; rapid.**
   ✓ **Any 1 of: uses non-renewable resources; higher operating costs.**

6. The Contact process is used to make sulfuric acid.*

a) Why might sulfuric acid be important? [1]

    Any 1 of:
    - ✓ **Manufacturing paint**
    - ✓ **Manufacturing detergent**
    - ✓ **Making fertilisers**

b) State three conditions needed for the conversion of sulfur dioxide to sulfur trioxide. [3]

    - ✓ **450°C.**
    - ✓ **2 atm.**
    - ✓ **Vanadium(V) oxide catalyst.**

c) Why is sulfur trioxide converted into oleum instead of directly reacting with water to form sulfuric acid? [1]

    - ✓ **It will produce an uncontrollable fog of concentrated sulfuric acid, which is dangerous.**

d) Give the chemical equation for the conversion of oleum to sulfuric acid. [1]

    - ✓ $H_2S_2O_7(l) + H_2O(l) \rightarrow 2H_2SO_4(aq)$

✓ SECTION 4: MANIPULATE

(Total: 38 marks)

These questions will require you to utilise what you know from multiple chapters of this section. Try your best!

1. Winter is coming and the Wildlings are running out of fuel for fire. They however, have lots of yeast and sugar cane.

   a) Suggest a suitable method that the Wildlings should use to make more ethanol - their source of fuel.* [1]

   b) Write an equation for your answer to part a).* [1]

   c) One of them feasts on some spare corn. Corn contains lots of starch, which is digested by the enzyme amylase, found in saliva. Amylase is a biological catalyst. Explain what a catalyst does and how it works. [2]

   d) Illustrate your explanation above by drawing the effect of the catalyst on this energy profile: [1]

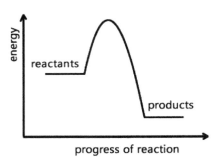

   e) Name the catalyst used in the hydration of ethene.* [1]

2. Nigel is a student at South Park Elementary and following his friend's advice, he decides to put some Mentos in some Coke. It explodes in his face.

   a) His teacher suggests (wrongly) that the Mentos somehow helps lower the activation energy. What is meant by the *activation energy*? [1]
   b) Nigel then cuts his Mentos into smaller cubes and puts them in a bottle of Coke. It explodes at a quicker rate. On the figure below, which shows how gas is produced over time, draw what the new curve might look like. [1]

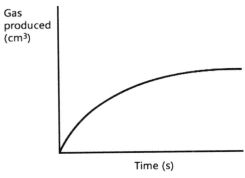

c) Explain why increasing the temperature might increase the rate of reaction. [2]
d) Coke cans are made of aluminium. Suggest one reason why aluminium is suitable for this. [1]

3. Some men just want to watch the world burn. Indeed, the Joker's next plot is to create artificial acid rain using sulfuric acid to wreak havoc on Gotham City.

   a) He first makes some sulfur dioxide. Write the balanced chemical equation for this, including state symbols.* [2]
   b) The equation for the next step is: $2SO_2(g) + O_2(g) \rightleftharpoons 2SO_3$

       i. State two properties of a system in dynamic equilibrium. [2]
       ii. What happens to the position of equilibrium if more O_2 is added? [2]
       iii. What happens to the position of equilibrium if pressure is decreased? [2]
       iv. State the temperature and pressure that are in fact used in the industrial manufacture of sulfuric acid.* [2]

   c) To prevent producing an uncontrollable fog of concentrated sulfuric acid, what must the Joker do with the SO_3? [1]

4. Professor Stark is giving a lecture on electrolysis at the University of Quahog. He electrolyses some copper(II) sulfate solution.*

    a) State two observations of the experiment. [2]
    b) Write the ionic half equations for the reactions occurring at each electrode. [2]
    c) He leaves the experiment for a very long time, and then drops some methyl orange indicator into the solution. What colour change (if any) is observed? [1]

5. Adamantium is a metal used by S.H.I.E.L.D. to make lots of different weapons. It is extracted in exactly the same way as iron. Adamantium forms a 3+ ion 'Ad^{3+}'.

    a) Describe the structure of adamantium. [1]
    b) What is a reducing agent? [1]
    c) Write an equation for the reduction of adamantium oxide to adamantium, using carbon monoxide. [1]
    d) The 'adamantium blast furnace' produces lots of silicon dioxide impurities. Suggest how these might be removed and write the chemical equations of any relevant reactions occurring inside the blast furnace. [6]
    e) Adamantium chloride is melted and electrolysed. Write the ionic half equations occurring at each electrode. [2]

SECTION 5:

CALCULATIONS

5.1: BASIC CALCULATIONS

Here, we will be learning to:

- ☑ Calculate the relative atomic mass of an element.
- ☑ Calculate the relative formula mass of any give substance.
- ☑ Calculate percentage yield and understand its use in calculating efficiency of a process.

✓ UNDERSTAND

We've decided to put all the calculations in one section just because it makes it easier to find! By now, you've probably seen some of this in class, but if not...

GOLDEN RULES

Remember **EWARU:**

Equation
Working (all of it!)
Answer (full from calculator)
Rounded answer
Units

Make sure that you give each of these elements in your exam to ensure you don't miss out on any marks, even if your final answer is incorrect. It is possible that occasionally there may not be an equation or units for you to give. Equally, sometimes your full answer may not need rounding, in which case you won't be told to do so.

THE RELATIVE ATOMIC MASS

The **relative atomic mass**, A_r, is the weighted average mass of an atom of an element, taking into account the abundances of its naturally occurring isotopes, relative to 1/12th the mass of an atom of carbon-12.

It is calculated by:

$$A_r = \sum \left(\frac{\text{\% abundance of each isotope}}{100} \times \text{mass number of each isotope} \right)$$

Example: Iron has two isotopes iron-54 (abundance of 8%) and iron-56 (abundance of 92%). Calculate the relative atomic mass of iron:

$$A_r = \left(54 \times \frac{8}{100} \right) + \left(56 \times \frac{92}{100} \right) = 55.84 = \textbf{55.8}$$

OUR TIP
Always write down the full answer to the question before then rounding. This way, if you make a rounding error, you will only ever lose one mark. What is more, if you have to use your answer in another part of the question, you should always use the full (correct to lots of decimal places), rather than rounded, answer.

THE RELATIVE FORMULA MASS

The **relative formula mass** M_r is the weighted average mass of all the individual atoms that constitute the substance, relative to 1/12th the mass of an atom of carbon-12.

This is calculated simply by multiplying the **relative atomic mass** of each element in a chemical by the **number of times** that element appears in the chemical formula of the substance.

Example: find the M_r of potassium carbonate (K=39; C=12; O=16):

Potassium carbonate is K_2CO_3,
In other words: $2 \times K + 1 \times C + 3 \times O$
Therefore: $2 \times 39 + 12 + 3 \times 16 = \textbf{138}$

PERCENTAGE YIELD

The **percentage yield** is a measurement of the efficiency of a process; in other words, how much product was produced in comparison with what would theoretically be predicted given the original input. It is calculated with the formula:

$$\% \text{ yield} = \frac{\textbf{actual mass of product}}{\textbf{predicted maximum mass of product}} \times \textbf{100}$$

Example: it was calculated that 17g of ammonia should produce 80g of ammonium nitrate. However, only 74g of ammonium nitrate was produced. Calculate the percentage yield of this reaction:

$$\% \text{ yield} = \frac{\text{actual mass of product}}{\text{predicted maximum mass of product}} \times 100$$

$$= \frac{74}{80} \times 100$$

$$= 0.925 \times 100$$
$$= \textbf{92.5\%}$$

✓ LEARN

1. Calculate the relative atomic masses for the following, correct to one decimal place:

   a) Lithium (^{6}Li - 7.6%; ^{7}Li - 92.4%) [2]

   ✓ $6 \times \dfrac{7.6}{100} + 7 \times \dfrac{92.4}{100} = 6.92 = 6.9$

   b) Boron (^{10}B - 19.8%; ^{11}B - 80.2%) [2]

   ✓ $10 \times 0.198 + 11 \times 0.802 = 10.80 = 10.8$

   c) Carbon (^{12}C - 98.89%; ^{13}C - 1.11%) [2]

   ✓ $12 \times 0.9889 + 13 \times 0.0111 = 12.13 = 12.1$

   d) Nitrogen (^{14}N - 99.63%; ^{15}N - 0.37%) [2]

   ✓ $14 \times 0.9963 + 15 \times 0.0037 = 14.0$

2. Calculate the relative formula masses of:

   a) $MgSO_4$ (Mg=24; S=32; O=16) [1]

   ✓ $24 + 32 + 4 \times 16 = 120$

   b) KBr   (K=39; Br=80) [1]

   ✓ $39 + 80 = 119$

   c) $K_2Cr_2O_7$ (K=39; Cr=52; O=16) [1]

   ✓ $2 \times 39 + 2 \times 52 + 7 \times 16 = 294$

d) $NaMnO_4$ (Na=23; Mn=55; O=16) [1]

✓ **$23 + 55 + 4 \times 16 = 142$**

e) $CaCO_3$ (Ca=40; C=12; O=16) [1]

✓ **$40 + 12 + 3 \times 16 = 100$**

f) $CuSO_4 \cdot 5H_2O$ (Cu=63.5; H=1; S=32; O=16) [1]

✓ **$63.5 + 32 + 4 \times 16 + 5 \times (2 \times 1 + 16) = 249.5$**

3. My calculations predict that I should be able to make 50.1g of ethanoic acid in a reaction, yet I've only actually made 39.5g. Calculate my percentage yield, correct to one decimal place:* [1]

✓ **$\dfrac{39.5}{50.1} \times 100 = 78.84 = 78.8\%$**

5.2: MOLAR CALCULATIONS

Here, we will be learning to:

☑ Be familiar with the moles as a unit (where one mole = the Avogadro number of particles).

☑ Carry out mole calculations involving molar concentrations and molar volumes.

☑ Work out the empirical formula of any given compound.

☑ Carry out experiments to determine the formulae of simple compounds.

☑ Calculate empirical and molecular formulae from experimental data.

☑ Carry out electrolysis calculations.

✓ UNDERSTAND

A mole is a measure of the amount of substance. It is a bit like saying there is a 'million' of this, or a 'billion' of that, but as we all know, atoms are a lot smaller and so we deal with massive, massive numbers.

In particular, one mole contains **6.02×10^{23}** (also known as the **Avogadro number**) of particles. This number is derived from the number of atoms in 12g of carbon-12.

It is quite easy to calculate the amount of moles in a substance:

$$\text{moles} = \frac{\text{mass of substance (g)}}{\text{relative atomic/formula mass of substance}}$$

Example: I burn 13.5g of aluminium completely in oxygen to form aluminium oxide, as shown by the equation below:

$$4Al + 3O_2 \rightarrow 2Al_2O_3$$

a) **Calculate the number of moles of aluminium (Al=27; O=16):**

$$\text{moles} = \frac{\text{mass}}{A_r} = \frac{13.5}{27} = \textbf{0.5 mol}$$

b) How many moles of Al_2O_3 will be formed?

The equation, like any chemical equation, shows the **ratio** of reactants and products produced. In this case, for every 4 moles of Al, 2 moles of Al_2O_3 are produced. We've only got 0.5 moles of Al so...

$$\frac{0.5}{4} \times 2 = \textbf{0.25 mol}$$

Basically we know that 4 moles of Al gives 2 moles of Al_2O_3 - a ratio of 4 to 2. By dividing the moles of Al by 4 and multiplying that by 2, we find out how many moles of Al_2O_3 that 0.5 moles of Al makes, given the 4:2 (or 2:1) ratio.

c) What is the expected mass of Al_2O_3 formed?

We know how many moles of Al_2O_3 are formed, now we just need to convert that back into a mass by bunging it in the equation:

$$M_r \text{ of } Al_2O_3 = 2 \times 27 + 3 \times 16 = 102$$
$$\text{moles} = \frac{\text{mass}}{A_r}$$
$$0.25 \text{ mol} = \frac{\text{mass}}{102}$$
$$\text{mass} = 0.25 \times 102 = \textbf{25.5g}$$

The **molar volume** of gas is the volume that 1 mole of any gas takes up at a given temperature and pressure. At room temperature and pressure (rtp), this is **24 dm^3 or 24,000 cm^3** (1 dm^3 = 1,000 cm^3). Basically...

volume occupied (cm^3/dm^3) = moles × molar volume (cm^3/dm^3)

Example (from above): I burn 13.5g of aluminium completely in oxygen to form aluminium oxide, as shown by the equation below:

$$4Al + 3O_2 \rightarrow 2Al_2O_3$$

d) **Calculate the minimum volume of oxygen (at rtp) needed to react with all the aluminium. Give your answer in cm³.**

We know from part **a)** that we have 0.5 moles of Al. We can tell from the above equation that 4 moles of Al react with 3 moles of O_2, so 0.5 moles of Al will react with...

$$\frac{0.5}{4} \times 3 = 0.375 \text{ mol of } O_2$$

Now we must convert that to a volume so:

volume = moles × molar volume = 0.375 × 24,000 = **9000 cm³**

THE EMPIRICAL FORMULA

The **empirical formula** is the simplest whole-number ratio of the number of atoms of each element that make up a compound. It can allow us to work out the molecular formula from experimental data. Some steps to take:

OUR TIP

Best way to master molar calculations is to practice, practice and then do more practice. **Eat, sleep, practice, repeat.**

1. Convert the given masses of each element of the compound into moles.
2. Divide all the resulting numbers by the smallest of the resulting numbers. This will give you a ratio.
3. Write it down in 'empirical formula' form.

If we're told the M_r of the compound, we can also use the empirical formula to work out the molecular formula of the compound:

ratio (actual compound/empirical formula) = $\dfrac{M_r \text{ of actual compound}}{M_r \text{ of empirical formula unit}}$

The ratio tells us how many times we must multiply the numbers of each element in the empirical formula to get the molecular formula.

Example: 6g of carbon reacted with 1g of hydrogen and 8g of oxygen.

a) **Calculate the empirical formula of the compound formed (C=12; O=16; H=1).**

It's best if we draw up a table...

	C	H	O
Mass reacted (g)	6	1	8
In moles...(mol)	$\dfrac{6}{12} = 0.5$	$\dfrac{1}{1} = 1.0$	$\dfrac{8}{16} = 0.5$
Ratio	$\dfrac{0.5}{0.5} = 1.0$	$\dfrac{1.0}{0.5} = 2.0$	$\dfrac{0.5}{0.5} = 1.0$

The ratio is 1 to 2 to 1, hence the empirical formula is **CH_2O**.

b) **Derive the molecular formula of the compound, given an M_r of 180.**

M_r of $CH_2O = 1 \times 12 + 2 \times 1 + 1 \times 16 = 30$

ratio $= \dfrac{180}{30} = 6$

OUR TIP

Check that your molecular formula has the same M_r as the one given in the question!

Multiply the numbers each element in CH_2O by 6...

$C_{1 \times 6}H_{2 \times 6}O_{1 \times 6} = $ **$C_6H_{12}O_6$** ... glucose!

The next page contains another example but involving the **water of crystallisation** (basically, the ratio of water molecules that gets locked, per formula unit, in a hydrated crystal). This time, we'll also show one way in which we can use an experiment to derive the chemical formula of a compound.

Example: Hydrated copper(II) sulfate crystals have a formula of $CuSO_4 \bullet xH_2O$. To find the mass of water, hydrated copper(II) sulfate crystals were heated in a crucible until they became completely anhydrous (i.e. just $CuSO_4$), as the water escaped the crystals. The data is shown below:

Mass of empty crucible (g)	20
Mass of crucible and crystals before heating (g)	24.99
Mass of crucible and crystals after heating (g)	23.19

a) **Calculate the masses of water and anhydrous copper(II) sulfate, correct to 1 decimal place:**

We know that the final mass is just the mass of the crucible and the mass of the anhydrous copper(II) sulfate so:

Mass of anhydrous $CuSO_4$ = 23.19 − 20 = 3.19g = **3.2g**

We also know that the initial mass contains the mass of the crucible and the mass of the hydrated crystals; but the final mass only contains the mass of the crucible and the mass of the anhydrous copper(II) sulfate. Therefore, the difference between both masses will give us the mass of water:

Mass of H_2O = 24.99 − 23.19 = **1.8g**

b) **Find x (Cu=63.5; S=32; O=16; H=1):**

In other words, find the ratio of $CuSO_4$ to H_2O - so we can use pretty much the same method as we did earlier with the empirical formula…

	$CuSO_4$	H_2O
M_r	159.5	18
Mass reacted (g)	3.19	1.8
In moles...(mol)	$\frac{3.19}{159.5} = 0.02$	$\frac{1.8}{18} = 0.1$
Ratio	$\frac{0.02}{0.02} = 1$	$\frac{0.1}{0.02} = 5$

$x = 5$ (the chemical formula is $CuSO_4 \bullet 5H_2O$)

So, what if you're given percentages (e.g. compound X is made from 15% carbon, 40% oxygen...etc.) then simply **write these percentages as reacting masses** (e.g. 15g of carbon, 40g of oxygen...etc.). You will still get the right answer!

Example: I heat some magnesium in a crucible such that all of it reacts with oxygen. There is a 66.67% increase in mass. Derive the empirical formula (Mg=24; O=16):

	Mg	O
Mass reacted (g)	100	66.67
Moles (mol)	$\frac{100}{24} = 4.17$	$\frac{66.67}{16} = 4.17$

So the ratio is 1:1 - the empirical formula must be **MgO**.

MOLAR CONCENTRATIONS

Concentrations of substances are given as x **mol dm^{-3}** (i.e. 'moles per 1 dm^3') which basically means that 1 dm^3 (or 1,000 cm^3) of solution contains x moles of substance dissolved in it. We usually work in cm^3 but we're always given concentrations in mol dm^{-3} so to convert between moles and molar concentrations:

moles dissolved in a given volume = volume (dm^3) × concentration (mol dm^{-3})

So, if you are given the volume in cm^3, rather than dm^3, simply divide the number of cm^3 by 1,000, remembering that:

$$1,000 \text{ cm}^3 = 1 \text{ dm}^3$$

Example: How many moles of HCl do I have if I pipette 25 cm^3 from a solution of HCl with a concentration of 2 mol dm^{-3}?

moles = volume × concentration

$$= \frac{25}{1,000} \times 2 = \textbf{0.05 mol}$$

OUR TIP

You have to convert your volume from dm^3 to cm^3!

This section tends to be hard because questions will ask you to manipulate the molar concentrations equation a lot. And these questions are worth a lot of marks!

Example: I titrate 40 cm^3 of 1 mol dm^{-3} HCl solution to react with some 0.5 mol dm^{-3} NaOH solution.

a) **Calculate the volume of NaOH required to react with all the HCl. Give your answer in cm^3.**

You have to write the equation first to know the ratios of reactants and products:

$$\textbf{HCl + NaOH} \rightarrow \textbf{NaCl + H}_2\textbf{O}$$

Calculate the moles of HCl in 40 cm^3 of 1 mol dm^{-3} solution:

$$\text{moles = volume} \times \text{concentration} = \frac{40}{1000} \times 1 = \textbf{0.04 mol}$$

The ratio of HCl and NaOH is 1 to 1 in the equation above, so 0.04 mol of HCl would require 0.04 mol of NaOH. Now we need to convert that to a volume:

moles = volume × concentration

$$\text{volume} = \frac{\text{moles}}{\text{concentration}} = \frac{0.04}{0.5} = 0.08 \text{ dm}^3 = \textbf{80 cm}^3$$

b) **The resulting NaCl solution is heated until only dry NaCl crystals are left. Calculate the expected mass of NaCl crystals (Na=23; Cl=35.5), correct to one decimal place.**

We know that there would be 0.04 mol of NaCl left as dry crystals. All we need to do is convert that to a mass:

$$moles = \frac{mass}{A_r}$$

mass = moles × A_r = 0.04 × (23 + 35.5) = 2.34 = **2.3g**

ELECTROLYSIS CALCULATIONS

There are two types of electrolysis calculation that you need to be able to do. The first step is always to **write the two ionic half-equations** (unless the overall equation is already given). This first type is quite simple, so we'll use a worked example:

Example: I electrolyse some molten NaCl. If 1.84g of Na is deposited on the cathode, what volume of Cl_2 gas is produced (at rtp) (Na=23; Cl=35.5)? Give your answer in cm^3.

Always write the ionic half equations:

$Na^+ + e^- \rightarrow Na$
$2Cl^- \rightarrow Cl_2 + 2e^-$

...and balance them by making sure both have the same number of electrons:

$2Na^+ + 2e^- \rightarrow 2Na$
$2Cl^- \rightarrow Cl_2 + 2e^-$

We can see that 2 moles of Na is deposited on the cathode for every 1 mole of chlorine gas on the anode. So let's find the moles of chlorine produced first:

$$moles = \frac{mass}{A_r} \qquad \frac{1.84}{23} = 0.08 \text{ mol of Na} \qquad \frac{0.08}{2} = 0.04 \text{ mol of } Cl_2$$

And now, simply convert that into a volume, using our knowledge of molar volumes:

$$\text{volume} = \text{moles} \times \text{molar volume} = 0.04 \times 24{,}000 = \textbf{960 cm}^3$$

The other type of calculation involves working out how much charge has flowed through the circuit, and relating this to the number of electrons that have carried this charge. To start, we must introduce a new quantity, the **faraday**.

1 faraday = 96,000 coulombs (C) = charge carried by 1 mole of electrons

Which means that...

$$\text{moles of electrons (mol)} = \frac{\text{charge flowing through circuit (C)}}{96{,}000C}$$

Sometimes you might be told the charge indirectly - in other words, you have to calculate it. We mentioned in the 'Electrolysis' section that an electric current is a flow of electrons or positive ions. What we're really saying is that an electric current is really just **rate of flow of charge**, measured in **amperes (A)**. It can be calculated by:

$$\text{current (A)} = \frac{\text{charge (C)}}{\text{time (s)}}$$

... sometimes you might see this second equation written as $I = \frac{Q}{t}$

Example: Consider the molten electrolysis of aluminium chloride. If a current of 32A flows for 5 minutes, how many grams of aluminium are produced (Al=27)?

As always, write down the ionic half equations. Since the question here is only focused on aluminium, we only need to see what happens at the cathode:

$$Al^{3+} + 3e^- \rightarrow Al$$

Find the total charge that flows around the circuit:

$$\text{current} = \frac{\text{charge}}{\text{time}}$$
$$\text{charge} = \text{current} \times \text{time} = 32 \times (5 \times 60) = 9{,}600 \text{ C}$$

Then find the moles of electrons:

$$\text{moles of electrons} = \frac{\text{charge flowing through circuit}}{96{,}000 \text{C}} = \frac{9{,}600}{96{,}000} = 0.1 \text{ mol}$$

We know that 3 moles of electrons give 1 mole of Al so...

$$\frac{0.1}{3} \times 0.0333... \text{mol of Al}$$

And finally, converting that to a mass:

$$\text{moles} = \frac{\text{mass}}{A_r}$$
$$\text{mass} = \text{moles} \times A_r = 0.0333... \times 27 = \textbf{0.9g}$$

Finally, always remember:

GOLDEN RULES

Watch your units - keep them constant during calculations. Remember that equations must use figures in the following units:

MASS in g
VOLUME in dm^3
CONCENTRATIONS in mol dm^{-3}
TIME in s

Unless asked to do otherwise!

✓ LEARN

••

1. The following questions are on simple molar calculations and percentage yield:

   a) What mass of Na_2O will I expect to get if I thermally decompose 26.5g of Na_2CO_3 (Na=23; C=12; O=16)? [If I only got 12.0g, calculate my percentage yield*.] [5]

   ✓ $Na_2CO_3 \rightarrow Na_2O + CO_2$

   ✓   Moles $= \dfrac{mass}{M_r} = \dfrac{26.5}{106} = $ 0.25 mol of Na_2CO_3

   ✓   0.25 mol of Na_2O also produced (1 Na_2CO_3 for every 1 Na_2O)

   ✓   Mass = moles × $M_r(Na_2O)$ = 0.25 × 62 = 15.5g

   ✓   [% yield $= \dfrac{\text{actual mass of product}}{\text{predicted mass of product}} \times 100 = \dfrac{12.0}{15.5} \times 100 = $ 77.4%]*

   (max 5 for triple science)

   b) What volume of H_2 will I expect to get if I drop 6.5g of K into a beaker of water, assuming all of it reacts (K=39; H=1; O=16)?* [4]

   ✓ $2K + 2H_2O \rightarrow 2KOH + H_2$

   ✓   Moles $= \dfrac{mass}{M_r} = \dfrac{6.5}{39} = $ 0.1666... mol of K

   ✓ $\dfrac{0.1666...}{2} = $ 0.0833... mol of H_2 also produced (2 K for every 1 H_2)

   ✓   Volume = moles × molar volume = 0.0833... × 24 = 2.0 dm^3

   c) How many moles of water will I expect to get if I reacted 3,000 cm^3 of oxygen completely in hydrogen (H=1; O=16)?* [3]

   ✓ $2H_2 + O_2 \rightarrow 2H_2O$

   ✓   Moles $= \dfrac{\text{volume}}{\text{molar volume}} = \dfrac{3,000}{24,000} = $ 0.125 mol of O_2

   ✓   0.125 × 2 = 0.250 mol of H_2O (1 O_2 for every 2 H_2)

d) What mass of $BaSO_4$ will I expect to get if I react 4.16g of $BaCl_2$ with Na_2SO_4 (Ba=137; S=32; O=16; Cl=35.5)? [If I only got 4.00g, calculate my percentage yield*.] [5]

✓ $Na_2SO_4 + BaCl_2 \rightarrow BaSO_4 + 2NaCl$

✓ Moles $= \dfrac{mass}{M_r} = \dfrac{4.16}{208} = 0.02$ mol of $BaCl_2$

✓ 0.02 mol of $BaSO_4$ also produced (1 $BaCl_2$ for every 1 $BaSO_4$)

✓ Mass = moles × $M_r(BaSO_4)$ = 0.02 × 233 = 4.66g

✓ [% yield $= \dfrac{\text{actual mass of product}}{\text{predicted mass of product}} \times 100 = \dfrac{4.00}{4.66} \times 100 = 85.8369 =$

85.8%]*

2. I pass hydrogen gas over some copper oxide to reduce it such that only copper is left in the reaction tube. My results are shown below. Find the empirical formula of the copper oxide compound (Cu=63.5; O=16). [4]

Mass of empty tube(g)	48.500
Initial mass of tube (g)	52.075
Final mass of tube (g)	51.675

✓ Mass of O = 52.075 - 51.675 = 0.4g
✓ Mass of Cu = 51.675 - 48.5 = 3.175g
✓ Using table for working:

	Cu	O
Mass	3.175	0.4
Moles	$\dfrac{3.175}{63.5} = 0.05$	$\dfrac{0.4}{16} = 0.025$
Ratio	$\dfrac{0.05}{0.025} = 2$	$\dfrac{0.025}{0.025} = 1$

✓ Cu_2O

3. A compound consists of 80% carbon and 20% hydrogen by mass.

   a) Calculate the empirical formula of the compound (C=12; H=1). [2]

     ✓ **Using table for working:**

	C	H
Mass	80	20
Moles	$\dfrac{80}{12} = 6.667$	$\dfrac{20}{1} = 20$
Ratio	$\dfrac{6.667}{6.667} = 1$	$\dfrac{20}{6.667} \approx 3$

     ✓ **CH_3**

   b) The relative formula mass of the compound is found to be 30. Write the chemical formula of the compound and name it. [3]

     ✓ M_r **of CH_3 = 12 + 3 × 1 = 15**
     ✓ **Ratio = 30/15 = 2**
     ✓ **C_2H_6 (ethane)**

4. Hydrated cobalt(II) chloride crystals have a formula of $CoCl_2 \cdot xH_2O$. To find the mass of water, the crystals were heated in a crucible until it became completely anhydrous. The data is shown below:

Mass of empty crucible (g)	22.30
Mass of crucible and crystals before heating (g)	25.87
Mass of crucible and crystals after heating (g)	24.25

Find x (Co=59; Cl=35.5; H=1; O=16) [4]

✓ **Mass of H_2O = 25.87 – 24.25 = 1.62g**
✓ **Mass of anhydrous $CoCl_2$ = 24.25 – 22.30 = 1.95g**
✓ **Using table for working:**

	$CoCl_2$	**H_2O**
M_r	130	18
Mass (g)	1.95	1.62
In moles...(mol)	$\dfrac{130}{1.95} = 0.015$	$\dfrac{1.62}{18} = 0.09$
Ratio	$\dfrac{0.015}{0.015} = 1$	$\dfrac{0.09}{0.015} = 6$

✓ **x = 6.**

5. What volume of 0.6 mol dm^{-3} potassium hydroxide solution would we expect to neutralise 20 cm^3 of 0.8 mol dm^{-3} sulfuric acid? Give your answer in cm^3. [5]

✓ **$2KOH + H_2SO_4 \rightarrow K_2SO_4 + 2H_2O$**
✓ **Moles = volume × concentration = $\dfrac{20}{1,000} \times 0.8 = 0.016$ H_2SO_4**
✓ **0.016 × 2 = 0.032 mol of potassium hydroxide needed**
✓ **Volume = $\dfrac{\text{moles}}{\text{concentration}} = \dfrac{0.032}{0.6} = 0.05333...$ dm^3**
✓ **0.05333... × 1000 = 53.33 = 53.3 cm^3**

6. I react excess magnesium with 40cm^3 of 0.125 mol dm^{-3} hydrochloric acid. All of the acid reacts, and all the magnesium chloride is filtered to remove any leftover magnesium. The resulting solution is diluted by adding 360 cm^3 of water such that the total volume of the magnesium chloride solution is 400 cm^3. Calculate the concentration of the magnesium chloride solution in mol dm^{-3}. [5]

   ✓ **Mg + 2HCl → MgCl$_2$ + H$_2$**

   ✓ **Moles = volume × concentration = $\dfrac{40}{1,000}$ × 0.125 = 0.005 mol of HCl**

   ✓ **0.005/2 = 0.0025 mol of MgCl$_2$ (2 HCl for every 1 MgCl$_2$)**

   ✓ **0.0025 mol of MgCl$_2$ in 400 cm^3 of solution after dilution**

   ✓ **$\dfrac{0.0025}{\frac{400}{1,000}}$ = 0.00625 mol dm^{-3}**

7. Consider the molten electrolysis of lead(II) bromide. If a current of 24A flows for 8 minutes, how many grams of lead are produced (Pb=207)?* [5]

   ✓ **Pb^{2+} + 2e$^-$ → Pb**

   ✓ **Charge = current × time = 24 × 8 × 60 = 11,520C**

   ✓ **Moles of electrons = $\dfrac{\text{charge}}{96,000}$ = $\dfrac{11,520}{96,000}$ = 0.12 mol of electrons**

   ✓ **0.12/2 = 0.06 mol of Pb (2 e$^-$ for every 1 Pb)**

   ✓ **Mass = moles × M_r(Pb) = 0.06 × 207= 4.66g**

8. In the electrolysis of brine, what volume of chlorine gas will I expect to produce if I run a current of 3500A flows for 20 minutes (Cl=35.5)?* [5]

   ✓ **2Cl$^-$ → Cl$_2$ + 2e$^-$**

   ✓ **Charge = current × time = 3500 × 20 × 60 = 42,000,000C**

   ✓ **Moles of electrons = $\dfrac{\text{charge}}{96,000}$ = $\dfrac{42,000,000}{96,000}$ = 43.75 mol of electrons**

   ✓ **43.75/2 = 21.875 mol of Cl$_2$ (2 e$^-$ for every 1 Cl$_2$)**

   ✓ **Volume = moles × molar volume = 21.875 × 24 = 525 dm^3**

5.3: ENTHALPY CHANGES

Here, we will be learning to:

☑ Understand that chemical reactions can be endothermic or exothermic, and represent both on an energy level diagram.

☑ Calculate heat energy change and molar enthalpy change.

☑ Investigate heat energy change using simple calorimetry experiments.

☑ Calculate enthalpy change using bond enthalpy data.

✓ UNDERSTAND

Enthalpy change describes heat energy change under constant pressure and is denoted by the ΔH (units: **kJ mol^{-1}** or **kilojoules per mole**):

- If $\Delta H < 0$, then the reaction is **exothermic** - heat energy is given out.
- If $\Delta H > 0$, then the reaction is **endothermic** - heat energy is taken in.

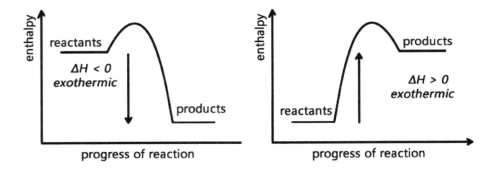

OUR TIP

Can't remember whether a diagram is endothermic or exothermic? Remember that exothermic means heat energy is given out, hence the products would end up at a lower energy level than the reactants. Similarly, endothermic means heat energy is taken in, so the products would end up with a higher energy than the reactants.

SIMPLE CALORIMETRY

We can calculate the energy required (in joules) for the change in temperature using the following equation:

$$Q = mc\Delta T$$

... where Q is the energy, m is mass (g/kg) of the substance absorbing the heat, c is the **specific heat capacity** (energy needed to raise 1 g/kg of substance by 1°C) and ΔT is the change in temperature.

There are many ways in which we can find these values:

- For combustion of a substance, we can use a **calorimeter** which is basically a device that transfers heat energy given out by a reaction sample to some water. The specific heat capacity of water is **4.2 kJ kg^{-1} °C^{-1}** and ΔT is the temperature change of the water. m is the mass of the water.

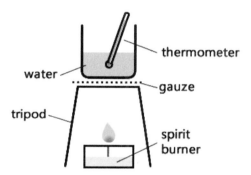

- For displacement, neutralisation and dissolving, we can put the reactants in a well insulated polystyrene cup (or suitable alternative) and measure the temperature change. The mass, m, is the mass of water in the solution, and c is assumed to be that of water (4.2 kJ kg^{-1} °C^{-1}).

Example: Calcium carbonate was reacted with hydrochloric acid. The temperature change and mass of solution were measured. The results are shown below:

Mass of CaCO$_3$ used (g)	20.0
Total mass of reactant mixture (g)	98.0
Initial temperature (°C)	23.7
Final temperature (°C)	31.1

a) Calculate Q to one decimal place:

We know that $m = 98.0g$, $\Delta T = 31.1 - 23.7 = 7.4°C$ and c is $4.2 \, J \, g^{-1} \, °C^{-1}$ so...

$Q = 98.0 \times 4.2 \times 7.4 = 3,045.84 = \mathbf{3,045.8 \, J}$

(**note:** c is $4.2 \, J \, g^{-1} \, °C^{-1}$ when working with grams, but $4.2 \, kJ \, kg^{-1} \, °C^{-1}$ when working with kilograms, so **WATCH YOUR UNITS**)

b) Calculate ΔH, giving your answer in kJ mol^{-1} (Ca=40; C=12; O=16):

So 20.0g of calcium carbonate reacts with hydrochloric acid to give a heat energy change of 3,045.84 J. But ΔH shows the heat energy change PER MOLE so:

$$\text{moles} = \frac{\text{mass}}{M_r} = \frac{20}{40 + 12 + 3 \times 16} = 0.2 \text{ mol of Mg}$$

$$\frac{3,045.84}{0.2} = 15,229.2 \text{ J mol}^{-1}$$

$\Delta H = \mathbf{-15.2 \, kJ \, mol^{-1}}$

(add the '-' sign because there is a temperature rise, hence the reaction was exothermic).

BOND ENTHALPIES

Bond enthalpies look at the energy change when bonds break or form:

- **Breaking bonds** is endothermic (you need to put energy in to break a bond).
- **Making bonds** is exothermic (energy is released when a bond is formed).

You can also calculate bond enthalpies using the following equation:

$$\Delta H = \sum \textbf{bonds broken} - \sum \textbf{bonds formed}$$

You will be given bond enthalpy values too!

Example: Work out the enthalpy change when 1 mole of methane undergoes complete combustion in oxygen:

C - H	C = O	O - H	O = O
413 kJ mol^{-1}	805 kJ mol^{-1}	464 kJ mol^{-1}	498 kJ mol^{-1}

Start with the equation:

$$CH_4 + 2O_2 \rightarrow CO_2 + 2H_2O$$

We can look at it like this:

$$
\begin{array}{c}
H \\
| \\
H—C—H \\
| \\
H
\end{array}
+ \quad 2 \times O{=}O \quad \longrightarrow \quad O{=}C{=}O \quad + \quad 2 \times \quad H—O—H
$$

Total bonds broken: 4 × C-H + 2 × (1 × O=O) = 4 × 413 + 2 × 498 = 2648
Total bonds formed: 2 × C=O + 2 × (2 × O-H) = 2 × 805 + 4 × 464 = 3466
ΔH = 2648 - 3466 = **-818 kJ mol^{-1}**

✓ LEARN

1. In an experiment, I take 1.5g of ethanol to heat 500 ml of water (assume 1 ml = 1 g). The temperature rises from 20°C to 45.7°C (For water, c = 4.2 J g^{-1} °C^{-1}).

    a) Calculate the heat change of the water. [1]

    > ✓ $Q = mc\Delta T$ = 500 × 4.2 × (45.7 – 20) = **53,970 J**

    b) Calculate the molar enthalpy change correct to 3 significant figures (C=12; H=1; O=16).* [3]

    > ✓ $\dfrac{1.84}{46}$ = **0.04 mol**
    >
    > ✓ $\Delta H = \dfrac{53,970}{0.04}$ = **1,349,250 J mol^{-1} = 1,349.25 kJ mol^{-1}**
    >
    > ✓ ΔH = **-1,350 kJ mol^{-1}**

2. Magnesium was reacted with hydrochloric acid, and the temperature change and mass of solution were measured. The results are shown below:

Mass of Mg used (g)	0.3
Total mass of reactant mixture (g)	50.0
Initial temperature (°C)	23.1
Final temperature (°C)	50.6

    a) Calculate Q [1]

    > ✓ $Q = mc\Delta T$ = 50.0 × 4.2 × (50.6 - 23.1) = **5,775 J**

b) Calculate ΔH, giving your answer in kJ mol^{-1} (Mg=24)* [3]

✓ Moles $= \dfrac{\text{mass}}{M_r} = \dfrac{0.3}{24} = $ **0.0125 mol of Mg**

✓ $\dfrac{5{,}775}{0.0125} = $ **462,000 J mol^{-1}**

✓ $\Delta H = $ **-462 kJ mol^{-1}**

3. Below are some bond enthalpy data (in kJ mol^{-1}):*

C - H	C = C	Br - Br	Cl - Cl	H - H
413	612	193	243	436
O = O	C - C	C - Br	Cl - H	O - H
498	347	290	432	464

a) Work out the enthalpy change when 1 mole of ethene undergoes an addition reaction with bromine water. [2]

✓ **$C_2H_4 + Br_2 \rightarrow C_2H_4Br_2$**

✓ $\Delta H = \sum$ **bonds broken - $\sum$ bonds formed = (612 + 4 × 413 + 193) - (347 + 4 × 413 + 2 × 290) = -122 kJ mol^{-1}**

b) Work out the enthalpy change when 1 mole of hydrogen gas reacts with chlorine gas to form hydrogen chloride. [2]

✓ **$H_2 + Cl_2 \rightarrow 2HCl$**

✓ $\Delta H = \sum$ **bonds broken - $\sum$ bonds formed = (436 + 243) - (2 × 432) = -185 kJ mol^{-1}**

c) Work out the enthalpy change when 1 mole of hydrogen gas reacts with oxygen to form water. [2]

✓ **$2H_2 + O_2 \rightarrow 2H_2O$**

✓ $\Delta H = \sum$ **bonds broken - $\sum$ bonds formed = (2 × 436 + 498) - (4 × 464) = -486 kJ mol^{-1}**

✓ SECTION 5: MANIPULATE

(Total: 32 marks)

These questions will require you to utilise what you know from multiple chapters of this section. Try your best!

1. Hannibal makes some vinegar to add flavour to his meat. Vinegar is actually ethanoic acid, with the chemical formula CH_3COOH:

   a) Calculate the relative formula mass of ethanoic acid (C=12; H=1; O=16). [1]
   b) He dilutes 12g of ethanoic acid in 40 cm^3 of water. What is the concentration of his solution? [2]
   c) The equation for the reaction between ethanoic acid and sodium hydroxide is:

   $$CH_3COOH + NaOH \rightarrow CH_3COO^-Na^+ + H_2O$$

   How many moles of sodium hydroxide are needed to just neutralise all of the ethanoic acid? [1]
   d) Thus, what volume of 0.4 mol dm^{-3} sodium hydroxide solution is needed to just neutralise all of the ethanoic acid? [2]
   e) Convert the sodium hydroxide solution concentration into g dm^{-3} (grams per 1 dm^3) (Na=23; O=16; H=1). [2]
   f) He places a conductivity tester in some spare ethanoic acid. What result does he expect to observe and why? [2]

2. A compound has a mass of 0.56g. 0.48g is carbon and the rest is hydrogen.

    a) Calculate the empirical formula (C=12; H=1). [3]
    b) If the relative formula mass was found to be 42, what is the chemical formula of the compound? [3]
    c) Calculate the enthalpy change using the bond enthalpy data below (in kJ mol^{-1}), if this compound undergoes complete combustion:* [2]

C - H	C = O	O - H	O = O	C=C	C-C
413	805	464	498	612	347

    d) In another reaction, 0.6 moles of CH_4 gas is burned completely in oxygen. Calculate the expected volume of CO_2 gas evolved.* [2]

3. S.T.A.R. Labs is investigating the energy changes of a newly discovered metal called 'speedium' (atomic symbol: Sp). It has an A_r of 222. They react it with hydrochloric acid:

Mass of Sp used (g)	2.2
Total mass of reactant mixture (g)	54.6
Initial temperature (°C)	24.0
Final temperature (°C)	35.7

    a) Calculate Q [2]
    b) Calculate ΔH* [2]
    c) Molten speedium(II) oxide is electrolysed and 25g of speedium is deposited at the cathode. What volume of oxygen is produced?* [3]
    d) In another setup, speedium(II) oxide is electrolysed using a current of 40A for 30 minutes. What is the expected mass of speedium produced?* [4]
    e) The % yield was only 68%. Calculate the actual mass of speedium produced.* [1]

SECTION 6:

THE EXAM & WHAT YOU NEED TO DO

6.1: COMMON MISTAKES

Here, we will be learning to:

☑   Avoid common mistakes students make - written from experience!

This will point out the most commonly made mistakes at IGCSE, so that you won't make them yourself.

Just reading through this won't help; you have to think about the mistakes, so you will instantly spot questions in your exam where you could fall into the same trap, and avoid losing marks.

✗   Common Mistake #1: confusing atomic number and mass number, or thinking mass number = number of neutrons

You will only make this mistake if you rush through a question, which says "How many neutrons are there in a sodium atom?" and put "23", because you think you are too clever for this question. **BUT**, although this may sound obvious, remember that this question is worth as many marks as the **hardest** one mark question on the paper, so get it right!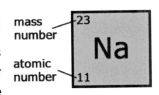

✗   Common Mistake #2: confusing group number with period number

The group number is the number of electrons in the outer shell; the period is the total number of shells surrounding the nucleus.

✗   Common Mistake #3: writing a balanced chemical equation when asked to write a word equation

When the question asks to: "Write a **word** equation for..." Don't write a **balanced** chemical equation. Not only is this harder, you won't get any marks for it.

163

✕ Common Mistake #4: messing up the chemical equation

When the question asks to: "Write a **chemical** equation for..." Don't:

- ✕ Write a word equation.
- ✕ Forget that some of the reactants or products may be **diatomic** (existing as a pair: N_2, O_2, F_2, Cl_2, Br_2, I_2, H_2).
- ✕ Forget to balance equations so that the numbers of atoms of each element in a reaction are equal on both sides of the equation.

✕ Common Mistake #5: confusing burettes and pipettes

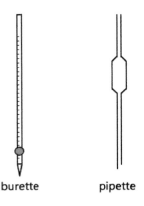

burette   pipette

✕ Common Mistake #6: misreading a burette reading

Two things:

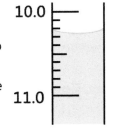

- The scale goes down from top to bottom, not bottom to top (as with a measuring cylinder).
- You read from the **bottom of the meniscus** (the curved line on the surface of the liquid).

So, in this diagram there is 10.25 cm³ (not 11.75cm³ if you read the wrong way, or 10.20 cm³ if you read from the top of the meniscus).

✕ Common Mistake #7: picking the wrong titration repeat readings

When given the results with repeat readings for a titration, and asked which repeats you should use, always **ONLY** use the repeat readings which give a "Volume added" within **0.1cm³** of each other.

For example:

Initial burette reading (cm³)	21.10	20.90	21.80	40.95
Final burette reading (cm³)	0.30	0.80	1.45	20.50
Volume of acid added (cm³)	20.80	20.10	20.35	20.45
Titration results to be used?	NO	NO	YES	YES

✕ Common Mistake #8: confusing isotopes with isomers

Remember:

- Isotopes are different forms of the same element with atoms which contain the **same number of protons, but different numbers of neutrons.** (They have the same atomic number, but different mass numbers.)
- Isomers are molecules that have the **same molecular formula, but different structural formulae**:

For example, C_4H_{10} has isomers - they have the same numbers of atoms, just arranged differently):

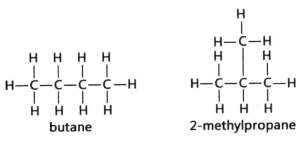

butane   2-methylpropane

× **Common Mistake #9: confusing alkanes and alkenes**

Remember:

- An alk**ane** is a **saturated hydrocarbon**, containing only single bonds, with the general formula C_nH_{2n+2}.
- An alk**ene** is an **unsaturated hydrocarbon**, containing a C=C double bond, with the general formula C_nH_{2n}. Alkenes decolourise bromine water from orange to colourless.

× **Common Mistake #10: confusing 'colourless' and 'clear'**

Something can be blue and clear (because you can see through it) **BUT** it is not colourless.

× **Common Mistake #11: giving a vague colour change answer**

When asked for the "colour change", you must give the **start colour** AND the **end colour**, otherwise you will lose a mark. For example:

"Phenolphthalein is put into acid. State the colour change when sodium hydroxide is added to neutralise all the acid."

- ✓ Colourless to pink
- × Pink
- × Colourless

× **Common Mistake #12: confusing physical tests with chemical tests**

If asked for a test for **PURE** water, the only, physical method is to test that the boiling point is 100°C and that the melting point is 0°C.

If asked for a **chemical** test for water, do not put 'boiling point 100°C, and melting point 0°C'. This is not a chemical test, it is a *physical* test. You must use either **cobalt chloride paper** or **anhydrous copper (II) sulfate**.

✗ Common Mistake #13: forgetting OILRIG

OXIDATION **I**S **L**OSS   **R**EDUCTION **I**S **G**AIN
(... of electrons)

For example, magnesium and chlorine react to form $MgCl_2$. Which substance is oxidised? Which is reduced?

- Magnesium is oxidised because it loses 2 electrons to the chlorine atoms.
- Chlorine is reduced because each atom gains an electron.

An alternative definition, and perhaps a more intuitive one, of oxidation and reduction is that of the gain and loss of oxygen. If a compound gains oxygen in a reaction, it has been **oxidised**. If it loses oxygen, it has been **reduced**, however, there is not always oxygen present, hence the previous definition.

✗ Common Mistake #14: confusing oxidising/reducing agents with OILRIG

Don't get them the wrong way round!

- An **oxidising agent** is something that gets **reduced** in a reaction.
- A **reducing agent** is something that gets **oxidised** during a reaction.

✗ Common Mistake #15: thinking (and writing down) that catalysts lower activation energy

They don't. They provide an **alternative route** for a reaction that requires a lower activation energy.

×   **Common Mistake #16: confusing the charges of the cathode and cations**

A reminder:

- The **cathode** has a negative charge.
- A **cation** has a positive charge.

If you ever forget, remember this: I used to have a girlfriend called Cath, she was a very negative influence. And: Cats are pawsitive.

×   **Common Mistake #17: messing up your graph**

When plotting graphs, take your time and be careful. At IGCSE chemistry, there is virtually always a graph to plot and it is worth between 3%-5% of the overall paper. It requires no knowledge and it is easy to get full marks on. The number of candidates who do not get full marks on graph questions would astonish you. The next section will ensure you never lose a mark on a Chemistry IGCSE graph question. If you are unsure about anything, there is a sample graph in Section 6.3 that should clarify each of these steps.

6.2: DESIGNING EXPERIMENTS

Here, we will be learning to:

☑ Answer questions regarding experimental design.

Questions which ask you to design an experiment are quite often worth 3-5 marks. Though you need the relevant content in your answer, there are a few tricks that can often help get some extra marks. Firstly, get your terminology right:

- **Independent variable:** the variable that is changed to see its effect on the dependent variable.
- **Dependent variable:** the variable being recorded as it changes due to the manipulation of the independent variable.
- **Control variable:** a variable that can affect the results of an investigation, which must be kept constant during the experiment.
- **Reliability:** how confident are you in replicating your data if you repeat the experiment? If you get similar repeat readings then your mean result is likely to be more reliable.
- **Accuracy:** how close is your reading to the real value?
- **Precision:** the number of significant figures it can be quoted to.
- **Validity:** is your experiment a fair test? Validity is the extent to which changes in the **dependent variable** are due to manipulation of the **independent variable**, rather than changes to other variables. For example, if you're investigating surface area on the rate of reaction, but you also change the temperature, your conclusion that increasing surface area also increases the rate does not hold much validity because you cannot tell whether it was the surface area or temperature that influenced the data.

OUR TIP

The distinction between precision and accuracy can sometimes be unclear. An example might clarify things. The Avogadro constant you use is 6.02×10^{23}. This is **accurate** because it is close to the real value but **not very precise** because it is only quoted to three significant figures. A value of 8.59384×10^{28} is more precise because it has many significant figures, but it is **less accurate** because it is less close to the real value.

> # GOLDEN RULE
> ## REPEATS ONLY IMPROVE RELIABILITY, NOT PRECISION OR ACCURACY.

Some ways of getting easy marks:

OUR TIP

An **independent variable** is one you change (e.g. temperature). A **dependent variable** is one that varies as a result of you changing the independent variable (e.g. mass of CO_2 produced). **Control variables** are those you keep constant (e.g. when testing temperature on rate, you must keep other factors such as pressure, surface area...etc. constant).

- ☑ **State how you would make your measurements:** to show that you know your apparatus e.g. "use a burette to titrate the hydrochloric acid...".
- ☑ **Carry out repeat readings:** to demonstrate that you recognise the importance of reliability.

Sometimes you might be asked why a reading or amount of product is not what you'd expect. Some reasons include:

- ✓ **Incomplete reaction** - not all the reactants have reacted with one another.
- ✓ **Inadequate insulation** - particularly for the calorimetry experiments, whereby heat loss from the system will influence the value of ΔH.
- ✗ **Human errors** - e.g. reading measurements incorrectly, spilling chemicals...Note that this answer **will never score you marks**, so don't use it in an exam!

You can usually improve your experiments by (though be wary of the context):

- ✓ **More repeats** - to improve reliability.
- ✓ **Narrower intervals** - e.g. testing for rate of reaction at 10°C, 20°C, 30°C, 40°C and 50°C rather than just 10°C, 30°C and 50°C.
- ✓ **More precise instruments**
- ✓ **Others** - this really depends on your experiment. For example, using an electronic laboratory water bath might produce more constant temperatures than heating a beaker of water with a Bunsen burner.

These are very generic ideas, so we recommend you do some of these questions from past papers and discuss them with your teacher.

6.3: DRAWING GRAPHS

Here, we will be learning to:

☑ Tackle the graph question.

☑ Use a pencil, not a pen

Use a sharp pencil instead of a pen. When plotting points or a curve, press lightly so that it is easy to rub out if you make any mistakes.

☑ Put the right variable on the right axis

If you have to use your own scale, make sure you put the correct variable (values) on the correct axis. So, if you have to draw a graph of time against temperature, and every 10 seconds you are recording the temperature of a substance, you need to put the time on the x-axis and the temperature on the y-axis. No matter what experiment you are given, there will be:

- One measurement (**the independent variable**) which the person doing the experiment will be changing by a certain amount. So, in the above experiment the person is changing the time by 10 seconds. This always goes on the **x-axis (horizontal axis)**.
- One measurement (**the dependent variable**) which the person will not know until they record the results. So, in the above experiment this is the temperature of the water (obviously we have no idea what the temperature will be!). This always goes on the **y-axis (vertical axis)**.

Label the x-axis and y-axis appropriately. If you get this section wrong you will definitely lose some of the marks for the graph question.

Temperature (°C)

Time Every 10s

☑ Take time working out the best scale

Once you have decided which measurement to put on each axis, you will have to decide your scale. This means how much each little square on the graph is worth. It should always be:

- **As much as possible**; you may lose marks if you do not use **at least** half the graph space.
- 1, 2, 5, or a multiple of 10. **NO MULTIPLES OF 3!!!**

The x-axis and the y-axis **do not have to have the same scale, and often should not.**

The x-axis and the y-axis do not necessarily have to start at 0. If the first value for temperature is at 22°C, it would make more sense to start the x-axis at 20°C. In fact, the below calculation for the value of *each square* will not work unless you start the x-axis and y-axis at roughly the lowest value in the dataset. This is the case in the example on **pg. 174-175.**

To work out your scale, use the following calculation:

$$\text{each square} \; = \; \frac{\text{highest } x/y\text{-axis value in table - lowest } x/y\text{-axis value in table}}{\text{total number of squares across or up graph paper}}$$

Round the value for each square up to the nearest appropriate multiple, e.g. if it were 12, make it 20, or if it were 6, make it 10. Use this value for each square to number each large square on the x-axis and the y-axis.

☑ Plot each line very carefully

Now plot each point carefully by:
- Going along the x-axis carefully using a finger (ensuring you are using the value for the independent variable not the dependent variable) and marking it with a small line on the x-axis.

- Going along the y-axis carefully using a finger (ensuring you are using the value for the dependent variable not the independent variable and that it is the value which corresponds to the x-axis value you have just marked) and marking it with a small line on the x-axis.
- Check to see if you have made a mistake on either value you have marked.
- Plot a point where the projections of the two marks meet on the graph.

Repeat this process for every point to plot from the table.

☑ Draw a line of best fit

Now look at the points you have drawn. They will either be approximately in a straight line, or a curve.

- If they are in a straight line, take a ruler and draw a line of best fit (i.e. if you measured the distance of all the points below your line from the line and added them up, then measured the distance of all the points above your line from the line and then added them up, they would be equal).
- This line does not necessarily have to go through any of the points you have plotted, nor may it necessarily go through the **origin**.
- Ignore any points which do not seem to fit the trend (the examiners usually have these in questions to try and trick you; they are called **anomalies**, and should be ignored completely when drawing a line of best fit). It is under your discretion as to which points are really anomalies, but they are usually very obviously separate from the rest of the data points.
- If the points are in a curve, draw a smooth curve in the general shape of the points plotted. Importantly here, **only** draw a curve if you know that the relationship between the two variables is as such. If this is not definitely the case, a straight line of best fit should be drawn.

So, here is an example which for you:

The experiment was observing the effect of temperature on dissolving sugar in water.

Temperature / °C	Mass dissolved in a minute / g min^{-1}
27	16
37	31
54	43
73	50
88	53
98	54

We have:

☑ Used a pencil.

☑ Put the temperature on the x-axis because that was being changed by the person carrying out the experiment and the mass dissolved in a minute on the y-axis because that was the measurement the person was taking.

☑ Worked out that on the x-axis:

$$\text{Each square} = \frac{98 - 27}{45} = 1.58 \approx 2$$

☑ Worked out that on the y-axis:

$$\text{Each square} = \frac{54 - 16}{30} = 1.27 \approx 1$$

☑ Plotted the points by marking along the x-axis and then the y-axis and drawing a cross where the two marks meet. (We recommend you use a '+' rather than an 'x' as a '+' does not get obscured when you subsequently draw your line of best fit, making the examiner's life easier.)

☑ Drawn a line of best fit, either a straight line or a curve, through the general direction of the points. Remember to ignore any anomalies (if there are any – there may not be!).

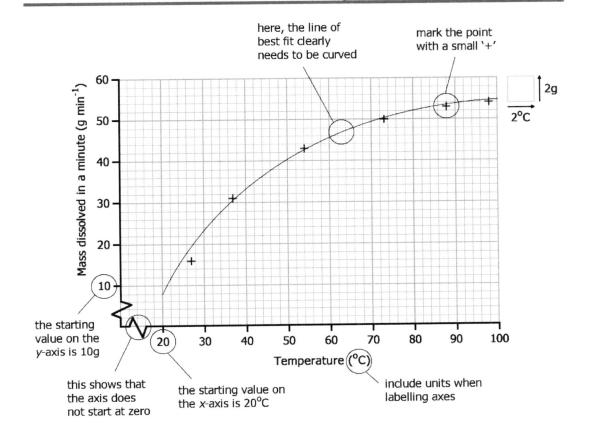

here, the line of best fit clearly needs to be curved

mark the point with a small '+'

the starting value on the y-axis is 10g

this shows that the axis does not start at zero

the starting value on the x-axis is 20°C

include units when labelling axes

6.4: THE GOLDEN RULES

Here, we will be learning to:

☑ Follow the Golden Rules... all placed on one nice neat page!

☑ Atoms 'want' a full outer shell of electrons to gain stability.

☑ You must include the charges (outside the square brackets) on the respective ions when drawing them out.

☑ When simple covalent substances melt or boil, it is the weak intermolecular forces between the molecules that are broken, not the covalent bonds. When giant covalent substances melt or boil, it is the covalent bonds that are broken.

☑ Balance charges for compounds.

☑ The number of atoms of each element on either side of an equation must be the same.

☑ When balancing equations (where the reactants and products are correct), you cannot add or remove reactants/products to balance the number of atoms for each element.

☑ Always state the initial colour and the final colour of the solution or precipitate if there is a colour change.

☑ When stating the location of the C=C bond or methyl group on the carbon chain, use the smallest number to describe it.

☑ Displayed formula - show all bonds.

☑ Catalysts do not directly lower the activation energy required for a given reaction to take place. They instead provide an alternative route for the reaction that requires a lower activation energy.

☑ Remember EWARU: Equation, Working, Answer, Rounded answer, Units. Make sure that you give each of these elements in your exam to ensure you don't miss out on any marks, even if your final answer is incorrect. It is possible that occasionally there may not be an equation or units for you to give. Equally, sometimes your full answer may not need rounding, in which case you won't be told to do so.

☑ Watch your units - keep them constant during calculations. Remember that equations must use figures in the following units: mass in g, volume in dm^3, concentrations in $mol\ dm^{-3}$, and time in s...unless asked to do otherwise!

☑ Repeats only improve reliability, not precision or accuracy.

APPENDIX A:

'LEARN' SECTIONS REVISITED

✓ Revisit Section 1.1: States Of Matter

(Total: 9 marks)

1. Describe the arrangement and movement, and draw the structure of particles in: **a)** a solid; **b)** a liquid; **c)** a gas. [3]
2. What is Brownian motion? [1]
3. How can you show that a sample of water is pure? [1]
4. What is the name of the process by which substances move from an area of high concentration to an area of low concentration? [1]

5. The following experiment is set up. Answer the following questions:

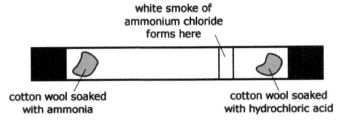

white smoke of
ammonium chloride
forms here

cotton wool soaked
with ammonia

cotton wool soaked
with hydrochloric acid

  a) Why would particles of hydrochloric acid and ammonia move towards each other? [1]
  b) The white smoke is formed when both substances react. Which substance (ammonia or hydrochloric acid) moves faster and why? [2]

✓ Revisit Section 1.2: Atomic Structure

(Total: 21 marks)

1. Explain what is, and give an example of: **a)** an element; **b)** a compound; **c)** a mixture; **d)** an atom. [3]
2. Fill in the gap. *The number of _____ must remain the same for the element to remain the same.* [1]

3. The diagram to the right was taken from a Periodic Table and shows information on silver:
  a) State the number of protons in an atom of silver. [1]
  b) State the number of neutrons in an atom of silver. [1]

108

Ag

47

4. Fill in the Table using the Periodic Table **(pg. 205)**: [7]

Element	Mass Number	Protons	Neutrons	Electrons
	106	46	60	
Silicon	28			14
	65	30		

5. What is shown by an element's: **a)** group number (if the element was in Groups 1-7) and **b)** period? [2]

6. Use the Periodic Table **(pg. 205)** to work out which element has 2 electrons in its outer shell and a total of 5 electron shells. [1]

7. Use the Periodic Table **(pg. 205)** to deduce which element has a combined total of 72 electrons and protons. [2]

8. Where in the atom are protons and neutrons found? [1]

9. State the relative masses and charges of an electron, a neutron and a proton. [6]

10. What do helium, neon and argon have in common about their outer electron shells? What effect does this have on their chemical reactivity? [2]

✓ REVISIT SECTION 1.3: SEPARATION METHODS

(Total: 9 marks)

1. Name a suitable method for obtaining: [4]
    a) Water from a table salt solution.
    b) Water from a mixture with any insoluble solid.
    c) An amino acid mixture, in which each amino acid has a different level of solubility.
    d) A miscible mixture of liquid hydrocarbons.

2. Kenny finds some impure copper(II) sulfate crystals which he wishes to purify. Describe the steps he should take to do so. [5]

✓ REVISIT SECTION 1.4: IONIC COMPOUNDS

(Total: 10 marks)

1. Draw a dot and cross diagram to show the ions formed after a reaction between sodium and oxygen. [2]
2. Draw the ionic lattice of NaCl.* [2]
3. Which of MgO or NaCl has the higher melting point and why?* [2]
4. Write down the chemical formula of the product from a combination of NH_4^+ and Cl^-; Na^+ and SO_4^{2-}; Al^{3+} and O^{2-}; and Cu^{2+} and NO_3^-. [4]

✓ REVISIT SECTION 1.5: COVALENT SUBSTANCES

(Total: 8 marks)

1. Define a covalent bond. [1]
2. Why is Cl_2 a gas at room temperature? Explain with respect to its structure and bonding. [2]
3. Draw the dot and cross diagram for methane. [1]
4. Why do diamond and graphite have such high melting points?* [2]
5. State a use each for diamond and graphite.* [2]

✓ REVISIT SECTION 1.6: METALLIC BONDING

(Total: 11 marks)

1. True or false? "The following elements are metals: **a)** boron; **b)** lithium; **c)** neon; **d)** rubidium; **e)** zinc; **f)** iodine." [6]
2. Describe the bonding in magnesium. [1]
3. Why can copper conduct electricity? [1]
4. Why are metals malleable? [1]
5. Why are alloys less malleable? [2]

✓ REVISIT SECTION 2.1: WRITING EQUATIONS

(Total: 15 marks)

1. Write down the chemical formula for the following: **a)** sodium carbonate; **b)** calcium oxide; **c)** iodine; **d)** aluminium chloride; **e)** ammonium hydroxide; **f)** potassium manganate(VII) (**hint:** manganate ion is MnO_4^-). [6]

2. Balance the following equations: [5]
   a) $H_2 + O_2 \rightarrow H_2O$
   b) $H_2SO_4 + NaOH \rightarrow Na_2SO_4 + H_2O$
   c) $Al^{3+} + e^- \rightarrow Al$
   d) $Li + HCl \rightarrow LiCl + H_2$
   e) $C_6H_{12}O_6 + O_2 \rightarrow CO_2 + H_2O$

3. Rewrite the following word equations as balanced chemical equations: [4]
   a) potassium + water → potassium hydroxide + hydrogen
   b) hydrochloric acid + magnesium hydroxide → magnesium chloride + water (**hint:** hydrochloric acid is HCl)
   c) calcium + water → calcium hydroxide + hydrogen
   d) sodium carbonate + nitric acid → sodium nitrate + water + carbon dioxide (**hint:** nitric acid is HNO_3)

✓ REVISIT SECTION 2.2: GROUPS 1 & 7

(Total: 18 marks)

1. State two observations when a piece of sodium is placed in a trough of water other than that it floats. [2]
2. Identify the ion responsible for making a substance: **a)** acidic or **b)** alkaline. [2]
3. Hydrogen bromide is formed in the following reaction: $Br_2(g) + H_2(g) \rightarrow 2HBr(g)$. It has similar chemical properties to hydrogen chloride. Hence, state the colour change of blue litmus paper when it is added to a *solution* of HBr. Give a reason for your answer. [2]
4. A sample of hydrogen bromide is dissolved in methylbenzene. State, with a reason, the final colour of the blue litmus paper when it has been added. [2]
5. State [and explain]* the trend in reactivity of Group 1 metals. [4]
6. State the colour and appearance of Cl_2, Br_2 and I_2 at room temperature. [3]

7. What is observed (if any) when $Cl_2(aq)$ is added to $KBr(aq)$? If a reaction occurs, write a balanced chemical equation for it (include state symbols). [2]

8. Write the balanced equation for the reaction between potassium and water. [1]

✓ REVISIT SECTION 2.3: OXYGEN & OXIDES

(Total: 11 marks)

1. Are metal oxides basic or acidic? [1]
2. Are non-metal oxides basic or acidic? [1]
3. Give two industrial uses of carbon dioxide. [2]
4. Write the balanced equation for the decomposition of hydrogen peroxide. [1]
5. Write the balanced equation for the reaction used to prepare carbon dioxide gas in the lab (include state symbols). Explain why collection by downward delivery is possible. [2]
6. On average, what % of air is made up of: **a)** N_2; **b)** O_2; **c)** CO_2; and **d)** argon? [4]

✓ REVISIT SECTION 2.4: HYDROGEN & WATER

(Total: 9 marks)

1. What substance can be used as a chemical test for the presence of water and what colour change is seen when water is present? [1]
2. Write the balanced chemical equation for the combustion of hydrogen, with state symbols. [1]
3. Write the balanced chemical equations for the reactions of magnesium, aluminium and zinc with hydrochloric acid. Include state symbols. [3]
4. Write the balanced chemical equations for the reactions of magnesium, aluminium and iron with sulfuric acid. Include state symbols. [3]
5. Why is the reaction between aluminium and hydrochloric acid initially slow? [1]

✓ REVISIT SECTION 2.5: REACTIVITY SERIES

(Total: 11 marks)

1. What is the chemical name for rust? What colour is it? [2]
2. What two substances must be present for iron to rust? [2]
3. State three ways in which one can prevent iron from rusting. [3]
4. If I try to react copper with dilute sulfuric acid, what will I observe? [1]

5. Write the balanced chemical equation for the reaction that occurs (if any) after I place magnesium in a solution of iron(II) sulfate. Include state symbols. [1]

6. From Q5, which is the oxidising agent and which is the reducing agent? [2]

✓ REVISIT SECTION 2.6: TESTS FOR IONS + GASES

(Total: 23 marks)

1. Fill this table for observations using the flame test: [4]

Metal Ion	Colour
K^+	
Ca^{2+}	
Li^+	
Na^+	

2. Describe how you would test for sulfate ions in a sample of sodium sulfate solution. Write a balanced chemical equation for the reaction. Include state symbols. [4]

3. When testing for halide ions, why do we need to add a few drops of nitric acid first? What step(s) do we take after? [2]

4. If we used the procedure from the answers to Q3, what will we observe for Cl^-, Br^- and I^- ions from the colourless solution? [3]

5. How would I show that ammonium ions were present in a solution? [3]

6. What happens if I place damp blue litmus paper in chlorine gas? [1]

7. I bubble CO_2 through limewater. Write the balanced chemical equation for the reaction that occurs (with state symbols) and state what is observed and why. [3]

8. I put sodium into a beaker of water. There is lots of effervescence. I place a lighted wooden split near the gas. State what I observe and write the equation for the reaction that produces the observation. [2]

9. How do you test for O_2 gas? [1]

REVISIT SECTION 2.7: ACIDS, ALKALIS AND SALTS

(Total: 27 marks)

1. What colour does universal indicator turn in: **a)** a strong acid; **b)** a weak acid; **c)** a neutral substance; **d)** a weak alkali; **e)** a strong alkali? [5]

2. I want to make some potassium nitrate.
    a) Suggest two reagents I can use. [2]
    b) What lab procedure should I use to obtain the potassium nitrate? [1]

3. I want to make some calcium sulfate.
    a) Suggest two reagents I can use. [2]
    b) Write a balanced chemical equation for the two reagents used in part a). Include state symbols. [1]
    c) What do we call this type of reaction? [1]
    d) How would we obtain the calcium sulfate from the rest of the products or excess reagents? [3]

4. Suggest two reagents I could use to make the following: **a)** magnesium carbonate; **b)** barium sulfate; **c)** sodium chloride; **d)** copper carbonate; **e)** potassium nitrate. [10]
5. Identify the reagent needed to make the following: **a)** sodium chloride from sodium metal; **b)** magnesium sulfate from magnesium oxide. [2]

REVISIT SECTION 3.1: ALKANES & ALKENES

(Total: 17 marks)

1. Give two features of a homologous series. [2]
2. Define an isomer. [2]
3. Draw the displayed formula for propene. [1]
4. Why are alkenes considered unsaturated? [1]
5. Describe the chemical test for alkenes. [2]
6. Write the balanced chemical equation for the combustion of ethane. [1]
7. Name the following compounds - some of them are challenging! [8]

a)

```
    H  H  H
    |  |  |
H — C — C — C — H
    |  |  |
    H  H  H
```

b)

```
        H
        |
        H — C — H
    H   |    H  H
    |   |    |  |
H — C — C — C — C — H
    |   |    |  |
    H   H    H  H
```

c)

```
    H  H        H
    |  |        |
H — C — C = C — C — H
    |            |  |
    H            H  H
```

d)

```
        H
        |
    H — C — H
    H   |   H
    |   |   |
H — C — C — C — H
    |   |   |
    H   |   H
    H — C — H
        |
        H
```

e)

```
    H  Br  H
    |  |   |
H — C — C — C — H
    |  |   |
    H  Br  H
```

f)

```
    H   Br
    |   |
H — C — C — H
    |   |
    Br  H
```

g)

```
  H        H
   \      /
    C = C
   /      \
  H        H
```

h)

```
    H  H  Br      H
    |  |  |       /
H — C — C — C = C
    |  |          \
    H  H           H
```

REVISIT SECTION 3.2: CRUDE OIL

(Total: 19 marks)

1. List the crude oil fractions in increasing boiling points, and state a use for each. [12]
2. What is the process of separation that occurs in the fractionating column? [1]
3. State two conditions needed for catalytic cracking. [2]
4. I cracked some decane. The products were ethene and ethane. Write a balanced chemical equation for this: [1]
5. How do nitrogen oxides and sulfur dioxide cause environmental problems and what can be done to alleviate these problems? [3]

REVISIT SECTION 3.3: SYNTHETIC POLYMERS

(Total: 7 marks)

1. Draw the displayed formula of, and state some of the uses for the following polymers: **a)** poly(ethene); **b)** poly(propene); **c)** poly(chloroethene). [3]
2. Why are addition polymers hard to dispose of? [2]
3. Name the two monomers of nylon.* [2]

REVISIT SECTION 4.1: RATES OF REACTION
. . . .
(Total: 6 marks)

1. The diagram shows the change in concentration of a product over time, and can be used as a measure of the rate of reaction:

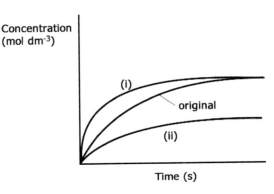

a) Which two factors might have been investigated to produce curves (i) and (ii)? [2]

b) What does a catalyst do and how does it work? [2]

c) How does temperature affect the rate of reaction? [2]

REVISIT SECTION 4.2: EQUILIBRIA
. . . .
(Total: 11 marks)

1. Consider the reaction: $NH_3(g) + HCl(g) \rightleftharpoons NH_4Cl(s)$ $\Delta H = -176 \text{ kJ mol}^{-1}$

    What happens to the position of equilibrium if: **a)** the temperature was increased; **b)** We remove the NH_4Cl as it is being formed? [3]

2. Consider the reaction: $3H_2(g) + N_2(g) \rightleftharpoons 2NH_3(g)$ $\Delta H = -92 \text{ kJ mol}^{-1}$

    What happens to the yield (amount) of NH_3 produced if: **a)** the temperature was increased; **b)** the pressure is decreased; **c)** adding a catalyst? [8]

REVISIT SECTION 4.3: ELECTROLYSIS

(Total: 22 marks)

1. Define: **a)** electrolysis and **b)** an electric current. [2]

2. I have two beakers. One contains potassium nitrate solution and the other is a glucose solution ($C_6H_{12}O_6$). I place a conductivity tester in each beaker. What would I expect to see and why? [3]

3. I electrolyse some molten zinc chloride ($ZnCl_2$).
   a) What do I observe at the anode and cathode? [2]
   b) What gas is produced at the anode, and how would you test to verify your answer? [2]
   c) Write the ionic half equations for each electrode (specify electrode), and state the processes occurring at each: [4]

4. I electrolyse some aqueous silver(I) nitrate.*
   a) What do I observe at the anode and cathode? [2]
   b) Write the ionic half equations for each electrode (specify electrode). [2]

5. I electrolyse some sulfuric acid - a diagram of this is shown right:*
   a) Label gases X and Y [2]
   b) Write the ionic half equations for each electrode (specify electrode). [2]
   c) Why is twice as much Y produced as X? [1]

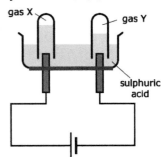

REVISIT SECTION 4.4: INDUSTRIAL PROCESSES

(Total: 34 marks)

1. Sodium hydroxide and chlorine are produced industrially via the electrolysis of brine, using a diaphragm cell:*
   a) Name a use each for sodium hydroxide and chlorine. [2]
   b) Write the ionic half equations for each electrode (specify electrode). [2]
   c) Why must hydrogen and chlorine be separated? [1]

2. Aluminium is also extracted using electrolysis:
    a) Explain the role of the molten cryolite. [1]
    b) Why do the carbon electrodes need replacing? [1]
    c) Write the ionic half equations for each electrode (specify electrode). [2]

3. The iron blast furnace is used to extract iron from haematite:
    a) Explain the role of coke and include two equations to show it. [3]
    b) Write the chemical equation for the formation of iron from its oxide in the blast furnace: [1]
    c) One of the impurities is silicon dioxide. Explain how this is removed. [2]

4. Fertilisers and nitric acid are made from ammonia.
    a) State three conditions used in the Haber process. [3]
    b) Why is it not profitable or practical to have a lower temperature? [1]
    c) How does iron affect the position of equilibrium? [1]

5. There are two methods of ethanol production used in the industry.*
    a) State three conditions needed for the hydration of ethene. [3]
    b) Write the chemical equation for the hydration of ethene: [1]
    c) Write the chemical equation for the fermentation of glucose. [1]
    d) State one factor that might determine which method of ethanol production is used in a country. [1]
    e) State one advantage and one disadvantage of the hydration of ethene over fermentation. [2]

6. The Contact process is used to make sulfuric acid.*
    a) Why might sulfuric acid be important? [1]
    b) State three conditions needed for the conversion of sulfur dioxide to sulfur trioxide. [3]
    c) Why is sulfur trioxide converted into oleum instead of directly reacting with water to form sulfuric acid? [1]
    d) Give the chemical equation for the conversion of oleum to sulfuric acid. [1]

REVISIT SECTION 5.1: BASIC CALCULATIONS

(Total: 15 marks)

1. Calculate the relative atomic masses for (to one decimal place): [8]
    a) Lithium   (^6Li - 7.6%; ^7Li - 92.4%)
    b) Boron   (^{10}B - 19.8%; ^{11}B - 80.2%)
    c) Carbon   (^{12}C - 98.89%; ^{13}C - 1.11%)
    d) Nitrogen   (^{14}N - 99.63%; ^{15}N - 0.37%)

2. Calculate the relative formula masses of: [6]
    a) $MgSO_4$ (Mg=24; S=32; O=16)
    b) KBr   (K=39; Br=80)
    c) $K_2Cr_2O_7$ (K=39; Cr=52; O=16)
    d) $NaMnO_4$ (Na=23; Mn=55; O=16)
    e) $CaCO_3$ (Ca=40; C=12; O=16)
    f) $CuSO_4 \cdot 5H_2O$ (Cu=63.5; H=1; S=32; O=16)

3. My calculations predict that I should be able to make 50.1g of ethanoic acid in a reaction, yet I've only actually made 39.5g. Calculate my percentage yield, correct to one decimal place:* [1]

REVISIT SECTION 5.2: MOLAR CALCULATIONS

(Total: 50 marks)

1. The following questions are on simple molar calculations and percentage yield:
    a) What mass of Na_2O will I expect to get if I thermally decompose 26.5g of Na_2CO_3 (Na=23; C=12; O=16)? [If I only got 12.0g, calculate my percentage yield*.] [5]
    b) What volume of H_2 will I expect to get if I drop 6.5g of K into a beaker of water, assuming all of it reacts (K=39; H=1; O=16)?* [4]
    c) How many moles of water will I expect to get if I reacted 3,000 cm^3 of oxygen completely in hydrogen (H=1; O=16)?* [3]
    d) What mass of $BaSO_4$ will I expect to get if I react 4.16g of $BaCl_2$ with Na_2SO_4 (Ba=137; S=32; O=16; Cl=35.5)? [If I only got 4.00g, calculate my percentage yield*.] [5]

2. I pass hydrogen gas over some copper oxide to reduce it such that only copper is left in the reaction tube. My results are shown below. Find the empirical formula of the copper oxide compound (Cu=63.5; O=16). [4]

3. A compound consists of 80% carbon and 20% hydrogen by mass.
   a) Calculate the empirical formula of the compound (C=12; H=1). [2]
   b) The relative formula mass of the compound is found to be 30. Write the chemical formula of the compound and name it. [3]

4. Hydrated cobalt(II) chloride crystals have a formula of $CoCl_2 \cdot xH_2O$. To find the mass of water, the crystals were heated in a crucible until it became completely anhydrous. The data is shown below:

Mass of empty crucible (g)	68.30
Mass of crucible and crystals before heating (g)	75.44
Mass of crucible and crystals after heating (g)	72.20

Find x (Co=59; Cl=35.5; H=1; O=16) [4]

5. What volume of 0.6 mol dm^{-3} potassium hydroxide solution would we expect to neutralise 20 cm^3 of 0.8 mol dm^{-3} sulfuric acid? Give your answer in cm^3. [5]

6. I react excess magnesium with 40cm^3 of 0.125 mol dm^{-3} hydrochloric acid. All of the acid reacts, and all the magnesium chloride is filtered to remove any leftover magnesium. The resulting solution is diluted by adding 360 cm^3 of water such that the total volume of the magnesium chloride solution is 400 cm^3. Calculate the concentration of the magnesium chloride solution in mol dm^{-3}. [5]

7. Consider the molten electrolysis of lead(II) bromide. If a current of 24A flows for 8 minutes, how many grams of lead are produced (Pb=207)?* [5]

8. In the electrolysis of brine, what volume of chlorine gas will I expect to produce if I run a current of 3500A flows for 20 minutes (Cl=35.5)?* [5]

REVISIT SECTION 5.3: ENTHALPY CHANGES

(Total: 14 marks)

1. In an experiment, I take 1.5g of ethanol to heat 500 ml of water (assume 1 ml = 1 g). The temperature rises from 20°C to 45.7°C (For water, c = 4.2 J g^{-1} $°C^{-1}$).
    a) Calculate the heat change of the water. [1]
    b) Calculate the molar enthalpy change correct to 3 significant figures (C=12; H=1; O=16).* [3]

2. Magnesium was reacted with hydrochloric acid, and the temperature change and mass of solution were measured. The results are shown to the right:

Mass of Mg used (g)	0.3
Total mass of reactant mixture (g)	50.0
Initial temperature (°C)	23.1
Final temperature (°C)	50.6

    a) Calculate Q [1]
    b) Calculate ΔH, giving your answer in kJ mol-1 (Mg=24)* [3]

3. Below are some bond enthalpy data (in kJ mol^{-1}):*

C - H	C = C	Br - Br	Cl - Cl	H - H
413	612	193	243	436
O = O	**C - C**	**C - Br**	**Cl - H**	**O - H**
498	347	290	432	464

    a) Work out the enthalpy change when 1 mole of ethene undergoes an addition reaction with bromine water. [2]
    b) Work out the enthalpy change when 1 mole of hydrogen gas reacts with chlorine gas to form hydrogen chloride. [2]
    c) Work out the enthalpy change when 1 mole of hydrogen gas reacts with oxygen to form water. [2]

APPENDIX B:

ANSWERS TO 'MANIPULATE' SECTIONS

✓ SECTION 1: ANSWERS

(Each mark is separated by either: '•' or ';')

Question 1:

a) A chemical bond formed from electrostatic attractions between oppositely charged ions.

b) A chemical bond formed from a shared pair of electrons between two nuclei.

c) Bonding in metals formed from electrostatic attractions between a lattice of positive ions, and the sea of delocalised electrons that surround it.

Question 2:

• Metals have delocalised electrons that can move.

• The layers of positive ions in the lattice can slide over one another due to its regularity.

Question 3:

• Sodium chloride.

• Because it is an ionic compound - electrostatic attractions between the NaCl molecules in the giant 3D lattice structure require more energy to overcome...

• Than those weak intermolecular forces between water molecules (whereby it takes on a simple molecular structure made up of covalent bonds, hence no ions are formed).

Question 4:

a) i.   ii.

b) Carbon; allotropes.

c) Giant covalent; a lot of energy needed (to break); the <u>many</u> strong covalent bonds that occur throughout the structure.

d) Weak intermolecular forces between each hexagonal layer (of carbon atoms each bonded to only three other carbons) so layers can slide off.

e) Very strong due to its giant 3D tetrahedral arrangement.

f) Simple molecular; relatively small molecules which do not covalently bond with one another to form a giant structure.

Question 5:

    a) $MgSO_4$

    b) $MgCl_2$

    c) $NaBr$

    d) CaO

    e) $CaCO_3$

    f) KNO_3

Question 6:

- Lithium loses its one valence electron to chlorine and forms an Li^+ cation, attaining a full outer shell in the process.
- Chlorine gains this electron and form a Cl^- anion, also attaining a full outer shell in the process.
- Electrostatic attractions bond the two oppositely charged ions together, forming the compound $LiCl$.

Question 7:

- Two sodium atoms each lose their one valence electron to one oxygen atom, each forming an Na^+ cation and attaining a full outer shell.
- An oxygen atom gains both electrons to form an O^{2-} anion and attain a full outer shell.
- Electrostatic attractions bond the two Na^+ ions with the one O^{2-} ion together, forming the compound Na_2O.

Question 8:

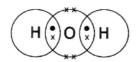

Question 9:

- Lots of energy needed to break the strong covalent bonds
- ... which consists of electrostatic attractions between the bonding pair of the electrons, and the nuclei of the atoms taking part in the bonding.

✓ SECTION 2: ANSWERS

▪▪

(Each mark is separated by either: '•' or ';')

Question 1:

- $H_2SO_4(aq) + Mg(s) \rightarrow MgSO_4(aq) + H_2(g)$

Question 2:

a) $ZnCO_3(s) \overset{\Delta}{\rightarrow} ZnO(s) + CO_2(g)$

b) $ZnCO_3(s) + 2HCl(aq) \rightarrow ZnCl_2(aq) + CO_2(g) + H_2O(l)$

c) No observation.

d) Limewater turns from colourless to cloudy/milky white.

e) Any 1 of:

- Blue cobalt chloride paper (turns pink).
- Anhydrous white copper(II) sulfate crystals (turns blue).

f) White precipitate forms.

Question 3:

a) Increases downwards; because the <u>number of electron shells increases down the group</u> such that the valence electron is further away from the nucleus; This means the electron is more weakly attracted to the nucleus, and so it is more easily lost.

b) Increases upwards; because the <u>number of electron shells decreases up the group</u>; electrons are more likely to be attracted to the nucleus to fill the valence shell (because the nuclear attractions act over a shorter distance).

c) $2KI(aq) + Br_2(aq) \rightarrow 2KBr(aq) + I_2(aq)$

d) Displacement reaction.

e) From top to bottom: sodium, calcium, aluminium, zinc, copper, silver.

Question 4:

a) Any 2 of:

- Ignite into lilac flame.
- Lots of effervescence.
- Potassium melts and disappears.
- Potassium spits around.

b) $2K(s) + 2H_2O(l) \rightarrow 2KOH(aq) + H_2(g)$

c) Blue or purple (either is fine).

d) Oxidation is loss of electrons; oxidation is gain of oxygen; reduction is gain of electrons; reduction is loss of oxygen.

e) Oxidised; lost an electron.

f) Lilac.

g) $Mg(s) + H_2O(g) \rightarrow MgO(s) + H_2(g)$

h) Enhances greenhouse effect/CO_2 is a greenhouse gas which can increase long wave radiation being trapped in the Earth's atmosphere/contribute global warming.

i) CO_2; <u>higher density than air</u> so it falls onto the flames and 'coats' it, preventing further combustion.

Question 5:

a) 21%.

b) Any 1 of:
- Iron wool in inverted test tube and measuring the % increase of water in the test tube after a given period of time.
- Burning phosphorus on an evaporating dish in a bell jar placed in a water bath, and measuring rise in water levels.
- Using two gas syringes connected to a containing with a sample of heated copper, oxidising the copper and then measuring how much gas is left in the syringes.

c) Manganese (IV) oxide catalyst; hydrogen peroxide solution; $2H_2O_2(aq) \rightarrow 2H_2O(l) + O_2(g)$

d) Fe_2O_3

e) Any 2 of:
- Coating in oil/paint/plastic/grease.
- Galvanising with a more reactive metal (e.g. zinc).
- Alloying the iron.
- Sacrificial protection.

✓ SECTION 3: ANSWERS

■ ■

(Each mark is separated by either: '•' or ';')

Question 1:

a) Gasoline or diesel.

b) Only single C-C bonds.

c) Any 3 of:
   - Same general formula.
   - Gradation in physical properties.
   - Similar chemical properties.

d) Add bromine water; no change observed.

e) CO; <u>reduces blood capacity towards carrying oxygen</u> because it binds to haemoglobin. Can lead to death.

f) Acid rain or smog; catalytic converters.

Question 2:

a) From top to bottom: refinery gases, gasoline, kerosene, diesel, fuel oil, bitumen.

b) <u>Fractional</u> distillation.

c) (Catalytic) cracking; alumina/silica catalyst; 600-700°C.

d)

i.

$$H-\overset{\overset{\displaystyle H}{|}}{\underset{\underset{\displaystyle H}{|}}{C}}-\overset{\displaystyle H}{C}=\overset{\displaystyle H}{C}-\overset{\overset{\displaystyle H}{|}}{\underset{\underset{\displaystyle H}{|}}{C}}-H$$

ii.

$$\overset{\displaystyle H}{\diagdown}\quad\overset{\displaystyle H}{\diagup}$$
$$C=C$$
$$\overset{\displaystyle H}{\diagup}\quad\overset{\displaystyle H}{\diagdown}$$

iii.

$$\overset{\displaystyle H}{\underset{\displaystyle H}{C}}=\overset{\displaystyle H}{C}-\overset{\displaystyle H}{\underset{\displaystyle H}{C}}-\overset{\displaystyle H}{\underset{\displaystyle H}{C}}-\overset{\displaystyle H}{\underset{\displaystyle H}{C}}-H$$

e)

$$H-\overset{\displaystyle H}{\underset{\displaystyle H}{C}}-\overset{\displaystyle H}{\underset{\displaystyle H}{C}}-\overset{\displaystyle H}{\underset{\displaystyle H}{C}}-\overset{\displaystyle H}{\underset{\displaystyle H}{C}}-H$$

$$H-\overset{\displaystyle H}{\underset{\displaystyle H}{C}}-\overset{\overset{\displaystyle H-C-H}{|}}{\underset{\underset{\displaystyle H}{|}}{C}}-\overset{\displaystyle H}{\underset{\displaystyle H}{C}}-H$$

Question 3:

a) Hexanedioic acid; 1,6-diaminohexane.

b) Condensation polymerisation; H_2O.

c) Poly(ethene);

d)

i. Poly(chloroethene).

ii. Bromomethane.

iii. Pentane.

iv. But-2-ene.

e) Inert or saturated.

f) Substitution reaction.

✓ SECTION 4: ANSWERS

(Each mark is separated by either: '•' or ';')

Question 1:

a) Fermentation of glucose/sugars.

b) $C_6H_{12}O_6 \rightarrow 2C_2H_5OH + 2CO_2$

c) Increases the rate of reaction without being chemically changed or used up; provides an <u>alternative route</u> of lower activation energy.

d)

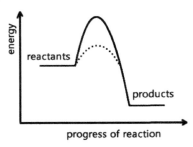

e) Phosphoric acid.

Question 2:

a) <u>Minimum</u> energy required for a reaction to occur.

b)

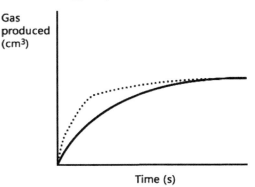

c) Increases kinetic energy of particles; hence increases frequency of collisions with energy $\geq$ activation energy.

d) Any 1 of:

- Low density.
- Malleable.
- Resistant to corrosion.

Question 3:

a) $S(s) + O_2(g) \rightarrow SO_2(g)$

b)

    i.   Any 2 of: Rate of forward reaction = rate of backward reaction; closed system; concentrations of reactants and products remain constant (also accept 'constant temperature').

    ii.   Shifts right; to reduce concentration of O_2.

    iii.   Shifts left; because backward reaction produces more moles (3 moles, compared to 2 moles in the forward reaction).

    iv.   450°C; 2 atm.

c) Dissolve in concentrated sulfuric acid to produce oleum.

Question 4:

a) Copper forms/coats the cathode; gas evolves at the anode.

b) Cathode - $Cu^{2+} + 2e^- \rightarrow Cu$; Anode - $4OH^- \rightarrow O_2 + 2H_2O + 4e^-$

c) Turns from orange to red.

Question 5:

a) Lattice of positive ions surrounded by a sea of delocalised electrons.

b) It gets oxidised/loses electrons.

c) $Ad_2O_3 + 3CO \rightarrow 2Ad + 3CO_2$

d) Add limestone; which decomposes to form calcium oxide; $CaCO_3 \rightarrow CaO + CO_2$; this reacts with the silicon dioxide to produce calcium silicate; $CaO + SiO_2 \rightarrow CaSiO_3$; which trickles to the bottom of the blast furnace and forms molten slag, which can be tapped off;.

e) Cathode - $Ad^{3+} + 3e^- \rightarrow Ad$; Anode - $2Cl^- \rightarrow Cl_2 + 2e^-$.

✓ SECTION 5: ANSWERS

■ ■

(Each mark is separated by either: '•' or ';')

Question 1:

a) **60** (no units).

b) $\dfrac{12}{60} = 0.2$ in 40cm³; $\dfrac{0.2}{40} \times 1000 =$ **5 mol dm^{-3}** (correct units given).

c) $\dfrac{12}{60} = 0.2$ mol ethanoic acid, so requires **0.2 mol** of NaOH.

d) $\dfrac{0.2}{0.4}$ (use of volume = $\dfrac{moles}{concentration}$); **0.5 dm³** or **500 cm³** (correct units given).

e) $\dfrac{mass}{23 + 16 + 1} = 0.4$ mol; mass = 16g, so **16g dm^{-3}**.

f) Light bulb does not light up; ethanoic acid does not dissociate into ions because elements are covalently bonded to one another.[1]

Question 2:

a) CH_2 (1 mark for correct answer; 2 marks for working)

	C	H
Mass (g)	0.48	0.08
Moles (mol)	0.04	0.08
Ratio	1	2

b) M_r of $CH_2 = 14$; $\dfrac{42}{14} = 4$; C_3H_6

c) $2C_3H_6 + 9O_2 \rightarrow 6CO_2 + 6H_2O$; $12(413) + 2(347) + 2(612) + 9(498) - 12(805) - 12(464) =$ **-3872 kJ mol^{-1}** (must be negative). (if answer to part **b)** is wrong, award 2 marks if error carried forward correctly)

d) $CH_4 + 2O_2 \rightarrow CO_2 + 2H_2O$; forms 0.6 mol CO_2 - 0.6 × 24 = **14.4 dm³** (accept answer in cm³).

---

[1] At least for IGCSE - ethanoic acid does dissociate slightly in solution to form CH_3COO^- and H^+ and therefore is a weak conductor of electricity.

Question 3:

a) $54.6 \times 4.2 \times (35.7 - 24.0)$ (use of $Q = mc\Delta T$); $= \textbf{2683.044 J}$ (correct units given).

b) $\dfrac{2.2}{222} = 0.0091$ mol of Sp; $\dfrac{2683.044}{0.0091} = \textbf{-270.7 kJ mol}^{-1}$ (must be negative).

c) Cathode - $2Sp^{2+} + 4e^- \rightarrow 2Sp$, Anode - $2O^{2-} \rightarrow O_2 + 4e^-$; $\dfrac{25}{222} = 0.113$ mol of Sp;

gives $\dfrac{0.113}{2} = 0.0565$ mol of O_2; $0.0565 \times 24 = \textbf{1.36 dm}^3$ (accept answer in cm^3).

d) $40 \times 30 \times 60 = 72{,}000C$; $\dfrac{72{,}000}{96{,}000} = 0.75$ mol of e^-; $Sp^{2+} + 2e^- \rightarrow Sp$, so $\dfrac{0.75}{2} =$

0.375 mol of Sp; $0.375 \times 222 = \textbf{83.25g}$.

e) $83.25 \times 0.68 = \textbf{56.61g}$.

APPENDIX C:

THE PERIODIC TABLE

The Periodic Table of the Elements

		1																0
		1 **H** hydrogen 1																4 **He** helium 2

Key:
```
relative atomic mass
   atomic symbol
       name
   atomic number
```

1	2												3	4	5	6	7	0
7 **Li** lithium 3	9 **Be** beryllium 4												11 **B** boron 5	12 **C** carbon 6	14 **N** nitrogen 7	16 **O** oxygen 8	19 **F** fluorine 9	20 **Ne** neon 10
23 **Na** sodium 11	24 **Mg** magnesium 12												27 **Al** aluminium 13	28 **Si** silicon 14	31 **P** phosphorus 15	32 **S** sulphur 16	35.5 **Cl** chlorine 17	40 **Ar** argon 18
39 **K** potassium 19	40 **Ca** calcium 20	45 **Sc** scandium 21	48 **Ti** titanium 22	51 **V** vanadium 23	52 **Cr** chromium 24	55 **Mn** manganese 25	56 **Fe** iron 26	59 **Co** cobalt 27	59 **Ni** nickel 28	63.5 **Cu** copper 29	65 **Zn** zinc 30		70 **Ga** gallium 31	73 **Ge** germanium 32	75 **As** arsenic 33	79 **Se** selenium 34	80 **Br** bromine 35	84 **Kr** krypton 36
85 **Rb** rubidium 37	88 **Sr** strontium 38	89 **Rb** rubidium 39	91 **Zr** zirconium 40	93 **Nb** niobium 41	96 **Mo** molybdenum 42	[98] **Tc** technetium 43	101 **Ru** ruthenium 44	103 **Rh** rhodium 45	106 **Pd** palladium 46	108 **Ag** silver 47	112 **Cd** cadmium 48		115 **In** indium 49	119 **Sn** tin 50	122 **Sb** antimony 51	128 **Te** tellurium 52	127 **I** iodine 53	131 **Xe** xenon 54
133 **Cs** caesium 55	137 **Ba** barium 56	57-71	178 **Hf** hafnium 72	181 **Ta** tantalum 73	184 **W** tungsten 74	186 **Re** rhenium 75	190 **Os** osmium 76	192 **Ir** iridium 77	195 **Pt** platinum 78	197 **Au** gold 79	201 **Hg** mercury 80		204 **Tl** thallium 81	207 **Pb** lead 82	209 **Bi** bismuth 83	[209] **Po** polonium 84	[210] **At** astatine 85	[222] **Rn** radon 86
[223] **Fr** francium 87	[226] **Ra** radium 88	89-103	[261] **Rf** rutherfordium 104	[262] **Db** dubnium 105	[266] **Sg** seaborgium 106	[264] **Bh** bohrium 107	[277] **Hs** hassium 108	[268] **Mt** meitnerium 109	[271] **Ds** darmstadtium 110	[272] **Rg** roentgenium 111								don't worry about this bit!

Values have been taken from 'Specification and Sample Assessment Material' booklet (Issue 5 – February 2015) of the Edexcel International GCSE in Chemistry (4CH0) website

BOOKS IN THIS SERIES

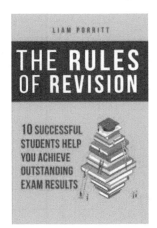

FOLLOW US ONLINE

Discover loads of useful resources and find out about all of our current and future products by joining the Exam Grade Booster community online.

Visit us: www.examgradebooster.com/gcsechemistry
to download our free chemistry cheat sheets containing everything you need to know, as well as our top revision and examination tips

Check out our blog: www.examgradebooster.tumblr.com

Follow us: @examgradebooster

Like us: Exam Grade Booster

Follow us: @examgradeboost

WRITE FOR US

| Want to become an author yourself? | Want to earn money? | Want to have something hugely impressive on your UCAS form or CV? |

Go to **www.examgradebooster.co.uk** and find the **Write for Us** page. This page should have all the information you are after, but if you have any other questions you can contact us via the website. In order to write for us, you will have to complete a very straight-forward application process (there is a short form to fill out at the bottom of the **Write for Us** page). Should you be deemed suitable to write a book, you will be given access to all of our manuscripts, formatting, cover design and branding as well as having the immediate advantage of working with people, just like yourself, who have succeeded in writing their very own books.

Do it:

- **Alone**
  ... It is possible; Liam wrote *Exam Grade Booster: GCSE French* while he was still at school.
- **With your friends**
  ... We have a number of books being written by groups of friends to lighten the work load.

Exam Grade Booster

Lightning Source UK Ltd.
Milton Keynes UK
UKOW07f1550130917
309122UK00003B/35/P